MW01167147

VISION

ADVENTURE

FAITH

By
Dr. R. Dean Lang

VISION, ADVENTURE, FAITH

Copyright © 2006 Dr. R. Dean Lang

All Rights Reserved

ISBN: 1-59352-194-4

Published by:
Christian Services Network
833 Broadway, Suite #201
El Cajon, CA 92021
Toll Free: 1-866-484-6184
www.CSNbooks.com

No part of this publication may be reproduced, stored in a retrieval system, or transmitted in any way by any means - electronic, mechanical, photocopy, recording, or otherwise, without the prior permission of the copyright holder, except as provided by USA copyright law.

Printed in the United States of America.

Dedication

I dedicate this book to my lovely wife Janice who has been by my side for more than 48 years. She is the mother of our nine children and my faithful helpmate in all ways. She is my secretary and still sits at the computer several hours each day. She is a great soul winner and wonderful with sign language teaching the deaf. Her encouragement keeps all of us going here at the Ranch. I owe any success that the Lord has given me to my dear wife. Thank you! We all love you.

Table of Contents

Dealing With Faith and Vision

Foreword

I am dictating this book eighty-five feet below ground at the Free Enterprise Mine in Boulder, Montana where I am for treatment for my arthritis. There is radium in the mine that as you breathe; it helps to clear up sinuses, lung problems, arthritis and many other things.

Since I am going to be here for another nine days, I want to take advantage of this time to write a book which, I've wanted to write, for many years. It is based on scripture. In Proverbs 28:13 it says *"Where there is no vision the people perish."* How important a vision is. A vision comes from a heart that is right with God to do the things of God. In James it tells us

"Where there is faith there will be works", and so this will be illustrated in this book.

Hebrews 11:6 says

Without faith it is impossible to please Him, for we must believe that, He Is, and that He is rewarder of those that diligently seek Him.

Yes, we must believe that He Is, and when we get that settled there is absolutely nothing impossible for God.

At this time I am in my 50th year of being a pastor and 30 years ago, I founded the Apache Creek Deaf and Youth Ranch near Apache Creek, New Mexico.

The story I believe will be humorous and sometimes cause you to cry and you will see where there is a vision it keeps people from perishing and it is only possible through faith and believing that He Is and that He is a rewarder of those who diligently seek Him. I hope you enjoy it, and that it will encourage you on to do great things for God, and may the Lord bless you.

Chapter 1

The Author

I was born on October 31st, 1935 in a farmhouse in Coles County, Illinois. My father's parents lived about a mile back across the field, and my mother's family lived a quarter of a mile down the road.

My mother was always a sickly woman and weighed less than 100 pounds, but I entered into this world 10 pounds plus. We lived in Coles County for a year while my father farmed there with his father. Then we moved north to a farm near Paris, Illinois, where we farmed on the shares for a couple of years. I have many memories during that time: of my mother pulling me down the lane in a little red wagon to check the mail, and of my brother and I playing in a sandpile alongside the house. I was the oldest of four children. My brother, Max, is a Doctor; my other brother, Teddy, is a military man, plumber, and in politics; and my sister, Carolyn, is a nurse.

When I was three we moved further north between Chrisman and Paris, Illinois, to a large 620 acre farm.

This is where I grew up and went to a one-room country school house called the Edgar School. It had all eight grades, and after eight years of listening to all of the classes recite each year, you should pretty well have it down. I remember that we walked a mile to school and had to cross a railroad track. It was during these school years that World War II broke out and train load after train load of jeeps would be on the trains. How I used to wish that one of them would fall off so I could drive the jeep back and forth to school! Often the train would run out of steam and have to stop at the water tower to take on water for the old steam engine, which blocked the road. We never told our parents, but in order to get to school on time we would have to crawl under the train, and run on to school. My father caught me driving the tractor to school one day when I was six, and told me I could only drive it when doing field work. The Taylor children lived just down the road, and when my brother Max started to school a couple of years behind me, we all walked together to school.

It was the teacher's job to go out and get the coal and build the fire in the stove in the back of the room. We would gather at school and sometimes help by pumping a bucket of water, which we set on a little table near the stove. The bucket had a dipper in it that we all drank out of. Soon the fire was roaring and the room was warm. The out house was in back of the school. The teacher's desk sat on the front right-hand side of the classroom with two or three chairs beside it. Each class, starting with the first grade, would come up, sit in the chairs and recite before the teacher, and then go back to their desks. There was a blackboard across the front where we would go to practice our spelling words. In the school we had 18 to 20 students.

When I finished the sixth grade, they consolidated the school district. We had to ride a bus to seventh grade at the grade school in Chrisman. When I went into the eighth grade, the 8th through 12th was all at the high school, and we had a little over 100 in all five grades combined. Our class was the largest class in the high school. There were 23 of us that graduated from that class in 1954.

During high school I started carrying my Bible to school every day. We got permission from the superintendent to hold a Bible Club in a classroom after we had finished our meal during the noon hour. However, one of the teachers complained and the state of Illinois said that it was illegal for us to do so. I remember the superintendent calling me into his office with tears in his eyes and saying we would not be able to meet anymore. He was a good man. Since we could not meet in the classroom, we would meet on the top floor in the hallway before school each morning. We would just happen to stop at a certain point to bow our heads and pray. It was not an official meeting, and I can remember teachers and students walking by, snickering and making fun of us. Someone said, "You must be a sissy carrying that red Bible on top of your books." I handed it to him and said, "Let's find out who the sissy is. You carry it for awhile." He refused and I said, "See it takes a man to carry it." That was the end of that conversation. At our 50th High School Reunion, many told me they remembered these things and respected us for doing them.

I was always very strong growing up, and worked hard on the farm. By the time I was six years old I was milking six cows every morning and evening, along with feeding the cattle, slopping the hogs and caring for the chickens. In the summer we would have the milking and the chores done, finish breakfast, and still be in the field by the time the sun came up. In the spring and fall I would work in the field, then jump over the fence, run the mile to school, come back home after school and get back on the tractor and work until dark. I enjoyed living on the farm and working hard, and to this day "fun", to me, is getting out and doing some hard work. I usually worked with the hired men, who usually complained that they had to work too hard to try to keep up with me.

One day when I was 15 years old after I got up, worked, went to high school, came home, unloaded a big truckload of limestone rock with a number sixteen corn shovel to fill in some muddy areas in the barn lot, and then went in and went to bed very exhausted. The next morning I got up and came down to breakfast and passed out, hitting my head on the sink and breaking my glasses. I was put back to bed and the doctor was called. In those days sick people did not go to the doctor; you called the doctor and he came to you. So he came and said I had had a heart attack. They rushed me to the hospital in Paris, Illinois, where they ran all kinds of tests and said that I had the arteries of a 90 year old man. For the next six months I was bed ridden for the most part. The next fall when I went back to school I was unable to climb stairs so that year and the next I could only take classes that were on the first floor.

By my senior year, I was much stronger and could climb stairs. I had to make up all the school work I had missed to graduate with my class in '54. For some courses, like typing, I bought a typewriter and a typing book and taught myself to type at home in the evenings. I finished up and graduated with my class.

From the time I was a little boy I planned on being a farmer when I grew up. I remember when I was six years old, I worked for a neighbor who asked me to cut out all of the burdock that was growing on his farm. After milking the cows each morning I would spend the rest of the day pulling my little wagon, digging down and getting the burdock out of the ground. I carried a little can of kerosene which I poured down in the hole to kill the roots. At the end of the day I would pull the little wagon up to the man's house and he would count the burdocks and burn them and give me a penny for each one. That summer I pulled up and destroyed 1200 burdocks for 1200 pennies or $12.

I told my father I wanted to get into the sheep business, so he took me to see a man that had sheep. This was back during the Depression when things were cheap, and I was able to buy four pregnant ewes for $3 apiece (thus my $12). Each of the ewes had either triplets or twins, and soon I had a lot of sheep. After a couple of years of this I sold those sheep and bought registered Hampshire sheep. I was in 4-H and wanted to have good sheep to show at the Fair. Once again my herd began to grow.

I had one sheep who would come running when I called. Her name was Mary. Before I knew this, I tried to drive the sheep. I remember once when a storm was coming, my father and I tried to drive the sheep into the barn. We would just about get them all in, then one would break and run and they would all follow. They were absolutely impossible to drive. Once I realized I could call Mary and she would come running and all of the other sheep would follow her it was so easy to control the sheep. If I wanted to put them in the barn I simply walked in the barn and called Mary, and they would all follow her in.

This became a valuable lesson later in life. We do not drive people, we lead people and they are willing to follow. Most importantly, Jesus Christ is our Chief Shepherd and we must learn to follow Him.

After I got my sheep business established I went to a sale and bought a very fine purebred Hampshire sow. She was to have piglets soon but I had only had her a few weeks when she up and died. I had paid $149 for this very special sow. Well, these are lessons we sometimes have to learn.

Once again I began saving up money for my sheep business. I did eventually get into the Hampshire hog business and always took blue ribbons on my sheep and hogs at the County Fair. Later on, I got into the short-horn cattle business. I rented pasture land that had barns on it and ten acres of corn that I grew for myself. I was raising about 500 head of hogs, had a large flock of sheep and a lot of cattle. By the time I was in high school I was clearing about $10,000 a year. Back in those days that was what a good doctor would make in a year's time.

From the time I was born on that little farmhouse in Coles County, Illinois, we always were in church every time the doors were open. When we moved to the big farm near Chrisman, a neighbor told our family that the Horace Baptist Church was about three miles down the road and invited us to come. Since we always went to church, we accepted their invitation. My parents were so surprised to find out that Pastor Golman, a man who had no legs but walked on his hands, was the pastor there. He was the man who had married them. We were always there, Sunday morning, Sunday night and Wednesday night.

I was a very bashful boy and had only one very close friend. His name was Dale Samford. Every Sunday we would alternate between going to our house where we would ride the goats or going to his house where we would shoot B-B guns and play in the haylofts. When I was nine years old we had a revival meeting with Evangelist David Cannine. Of course, we were there every night. It was Friday of the second week and Dale had gotten saved early in the revival meeting. Each night the conviction for me grew worse. I kept thinking to myself, "I will always go to church, I will give, I will help support missionaries around the world," but I was just too bashful to step out to receive Christ as Savior.

We were sitting in the very last row of the church over in the far left-hand corner. I was so convicted when Dale learned over and said, "Ain't you ever going to get saved?" It seemed that my life rushed before me. Yes, I would always go to church, and be active in it. But I would grow old and die and then I would go to Hell.

I said to myself, "I am not going to go to Hell because I am bashful," and I stepped out and went down to the altar where someone took the Bible, and among other verses read to me John 3:16. That evening I received Jesus Christ as my Lord and Savior. A few weeks later I was baptized and began to really grow in the Lord.

I had made up my mind that at six years of age I was going to be a farmer and was well on my way. The fact is, even in high school I had different landlords saying they would rent me their farms when I graduated. I had money that I could buy machinery with and in my senior year was elected most outstanding FFA (Future Farmers of America) for the state of Illinois.

However, one day out in the hog lot, I had become so convicted that God was calling me to preach. When I went in that evening, I called my pastor and asked him if he would meet me at the hog lot the next day after school.

I was busy slopping the hogs when he drove up. I told him that God had called me to preach. He said "fine."

I said, "I am too bashful."

He said, "Well then, don't!"

I said, "Well if I don't, then I will die."

He said, "Well, it looks like you will either preach or die," and got in his car and left. I don't mean to say that he was hard-hearted because Pastor Sibert was a real godly man.

The following Sunday after the service the Pastor asked me if I would go to the jail with him and a group of young people that afternoon. He said he had asked the young people to go along and sing a song before the service. I said, "You know I can't sing."

He said, "I know. Just move your lips and they will think you are singing." So I went with them. After the song, he got up and I thought he was going to preach. He said, "God has called one of our young men to preach this week and he will bring the message at this time." Wow, if he had asked me before, I would have been too bashful to have gone. My mind was blank except for John 3:16, the first verse I had ever learned in Sunday school at Horace Baptist Church. I remember turning to John 3:16 and preaching that day in the Edgar County Jail; five men received Christ as their Savior. I have been preaching ever since, and the burden for preaching has grown greater and greater.

I went to a pawn shop in Terre Haute, Indiana, bought an old public address system with a microphone and set up on the courthouse lawn. The sheriff had given me permission to plug into the courthouse. If I had some young people who would come and sing I would have them sing a song or two. If not, I had a turntable and I would play a gospel record and then I would stand up and preach. Back in those days absolutely everybody went to town on

Saturday night. You would sell your eggs and cream, then go to Kroger or IGA (my wife-to-be's father's store) and buy your groceries.

The custom was that after that everyone put the food in their cars, they would walk around the square: in one store, down the right aisle, across the back, up the left aisle and out the door. Then they would go on to the next store all around the court house square. So virtually everyone in the county would be in town on Saturday night. Afterwards I preached, and with the speakers everyone around the square could hear me. Out of my own money I bought boxes of gospel tracts and had a stamp made with our church's name on it. I would stamp the tracts and go around the square giving out tracts, witnessing to people and winning people to Christ.

This went on every Saturday night. Sometimes on Friday nights I would go to Chrisman, Illinois, where the stores were open on Friday evenings, and do the same. Sometimes on Mondays I would go to Terre Haute, Indiana, as their stores were open on Monday nights. I could not use the public address system there but I could stand on the street corner and preach, and walk up and down the streets giving out gospel tracts.

I graduated from high school in 1954 and that fall I enrolled in Bob Jones University. Every weekend I was out preaching. I would go to a town called Laurens, South Carolina, where from early in the morning until dark I would walk up and down streets in the black section of town and call, "You all come!" Children would come, and sometimes adults would gather under a tree. I would give a Bible lesson, sometimes with flannelgraph but always from the Word of God, and an invitation.

At first nothing much was happening. I would wear white buck shoes and a white jacket. Little children wanted to come and climb onto my lap. Often they had not bathed, their noses were running and it bothered me. But after a couple of weeks of that, I got a real burden and throughout the next nine months I saw 180 people come to know Jesus Christ as their Savior. Often when noon time would come, one of the black mamma's would say, "Preacher, come on in and eat with us," and I would have a fine meal with them. After spending all day going block by block, I'd have a class on the other side of town for white teenagers and sometimes a big youth rally on Saturday night.

On Sunday, I would go to Union, South Carolina, where I would preach in the jails, to chain gangs, on street corners, etc. The next year a church in Greenville that was just getting started asked me to come and help them on Sundays. Even before going to college I would preach in churches around the community as well as occasionally in our home church. There was a circuit that had five Methodist churches and often did not have a pastor to care for all five of them. They would ask me to come and preach in different ones.

There was a church at Borton, Illinois, which was maybe 35 miles from where we lived. When I came home from college the first year, they had heard that there was a preacher boy, and they asked if I would come and be their pastor. I preached there Sunday mornings and nights and Wednesday nights throughout the summer and whenever I was home from school. I would write letters to them when I was away and sometimes send tapes, etc.

The whole time I was at Bob Jones University I had very poor health. I had to eat at a special diet table and was under treatment. My junior year, after returning to college from being home at Christmas, my health was really failing. One day my brother walked into the room and found me unconscious. When I woke up, I was in the University hospital. I remained in the hospital there for more than a month and it seemed I was not going to get well. Previously, I had bought an old ambulance and put rows of seats in to take others out with me to preach. My father flew down to Greenville, took out the seats, put the cot in and took me home to Illinois. From there I went to Methodist Hospital in Indianapolis, Indiana, where they were originally going to operate, but then said it was useless and sent me home to die. However, God had other plans, and I survived.

During that time a group of young people from the Horace Baptist Church came to see me. My Dad had bought his uncle's farm near Westfield, Illinois, during the fall of 1954. I had spent a good part of the summer of 1955 working on it: adding bathrooms, cabinets, sinks, etc., as it did not have any of these. The group of young people came about 50 miles to see me, and I was flat on my back in bed. When they walked into the room there was one young lady that caught my attention. I knew who she was; her name was Janice Barker. She was born in Rockville, Indiana on the

Wabash River, January 8th, 1939. After they moved to Paris, Illinois her father owned the IGA Store. I remembered seeing her as a little girl when we had gone to her church in Paris, Illinois, for special revival meetings. When Pastor Sibert had announced that I was in the hospital, at Bob Jones University, and asked people to send me a card and pray for me, she had sent me a card of encouragement. I could not get her out of my mind.

Finally, I began to get better. Dr. Newlin found that there was a pinched nerve in my back causing acid to pour into my stomach. The doctor did much to improve this and I slowly regained my health. Janice was graduating from Paris High School in Paris, Illinois. The church, in place of the prom, had a banquet for their teens and she invited me to go with her as her guest. From then on we were dating. Even though I was not well enough to return in the Fall, I was pastoring the Borton Church full-time so I asked her to marry me. We were married on September 22, 1957.

We bought a house trailer and lived in Paris, Illinois. I would drive about 20 miles to the Borton Church and preach Sunday mornings and nights and Wednesday nights. There was a church about 20 miles to the east in Indiana, and they asked if I would come and preach for them, so finally I agreed to preach there on Sunday nights and Thursday nights and at the Borton Church on Sunday mornings and Wednesday nights. This went on for about another year, and then the church in Shepardsville, Indiana, wanted us to come full-time, so we moved to Indiana and I became the full-time pastor there.

My health was still up and down. Shepardsville, Indiana, was an area where there were many abandoned coal mines and there was a gas escaping out of them called black damp. My asthma became very severe and my heart trouble got worse. Finally my doctor told me that I either had to move to a different area or I would move out in a pine box. Sadly, the doctor did not take his own advice and he left in a pine box a few years later.

In 1960, we moved to northern Illinois, to a place called Harrison. It was north of Rockford, almost on the Wisconsin line. I was pastor there for five years. The church grew and grew and built us a parsonage. I wanted to stay there forever.

One Sunday evening there were three men in the service and I thought they were fishermen. We lived on the Pecatonica River and it was common to see fishermen. After service, they asked if they could talk with me. We invited them over to the parsonage and they said they wanted me to come and be their pastor in Dwight, Illinois. I let them know that I was not interested at all. For five years we had received a salary of $35 a week and now the church had just built us a new parsonage and was paying us $50 a week. But that was not the determining factor. I had won most of the people in the church to Jesus Christ and had no desire to leave.

They continued to call and ask if I would come. They told me they had led a young couple to the Lord and asked if I would come and baptize them and preach on Sunday. I told them no, I had my own church to preach at on Sunday. Then they asked if I would come on a Wednesday night and preach for them and baptize the couple. I said "No, I preach at my own church on Wednesday."

Finally, out of desperation, they called me and asked if I would come on a Friday night and preach for them and baptize this young couple. I consented and drove the 150 miles, which seemed an eternity away, and preached to them on Friday night. It was a small church of about 15 people and we went to the basement where they had a horse tank. I stood beside the horse tank and baptized the man and his wife. Again, they asked me if I would become their pastor and I said "no."

On the way back home the Lord began to speak to my heart and said, "That is where I want you to go."

After much prayer I finally said, "Lord, let's make this difficult. I have to know for sure that this is where you want me to be." I had been in Harrison for five years and wanted to stay for the rest of my life. I said, "If they call back and say they have voted unanimously to call me, even though I told them I would not come, and if they will ask me to preach a two-week revival myself as soon as I get there, I will know it is your calling." Well, Wednesday night after church we went home and the phone rang. They said, "We had a special business meeting tonight and even though you said you would not come, we voted unanimously to call you as our pastor." They also said, "We would like you to preach a two-week revival as soon as you get here."

I said "Well, you got me," and I told them about the

fleece I had laid out before the Lord.

They said, "How soon can you come?"

I said, "Not for three months." They asked why three months, and I said, "Though this church is over 75 years old, I am the first full-time pastor they have ever had and I will not leave until I find them another pastor. I need three months to make sure this is all taken care of." At the end of three months the church had called a pastor. I asked them to pay him $75 a week instead of the $50 they had been paying us, and they were ready to move into the new parsonage.

At the church in Dwight, Elmer owned a construction business and he sent his semi-dump truck up to load our furniture. It was a round-bottom semi-dump and very rough riding. Our folks there at the church were very upset. They said, "Not only did they steal our preacher, but they came to move him in a dump truck." Well, we loaded up what we had and headed for Dwight. We arrived there on Wednesday evening. I had written ahead and asked if they could find a place for us to rent where we could live. They had never answered our letter, so we had no idea when we left Harrison where we would be living in Dwight. We arrived and they had prepared some food for us at the church, and then it was time for a regular monthly Wednesday business meeting. After I preached, they called the meeting to order and read the minutes of the last meeting. In the minutes they stated that they had just bought a parsonage for the new pastor, a big two-story house, and that they were going to pay him $150 a week. My wife and I sat there with our mouths open, aghast. We thought for sure we would go back at least to $35 dollars a week. They as other churches had, asked what we wanted for a salary, and we said, as we have always said, "We work for the Lord, that would be between you and the Lord."

We stayed with a family, and the next morning they moved our furniture into the big two-story parsonage. We got everything settled and announced Sunday morning that our revival meeting would start. I had gotten some flyers and passed them out through the community. I preached Sunday morning and Sunday night and Monday night to the Christians, who really got burdened for souls and got on fire. It was the nearest thing to great revival that I have ever seen.

The man who had sent the dump truck for us had told me that until I got established I could just come out to his ready-mix yard and he would fill my car up with gas. I drove in Tuesday morning and no one was around. He was there locking the door. I said, "Oh, are you locked up?"

He said, "No, I will turn the pump on for you."

I said, "Where is everybody?"

He said "Everybody came to work this morning, and said, 'Brother Riber, we've just got to go soul winning. We can't just sit back and work today.'" He said, "I feel the same way, so we have closed up shop and we are all going soul winning." Well, by the end of the two weeks the church was so packed, that half of the people were standing around the walls, down the center aisle, in the vestibule, and I even had people standing on the platform so they could hear. There was not room for me to move, but to just stand still. In 2 ½ weeks we had grown from 15 to 200.

On Wednesday night, following the two-week revival, someone said, "I make a motion we build the church bigger."

Someone else said, "I second that," and everybody raised their hands. Well, I went ahead and preached that evening. Thursday morning I was at the church, praying (our office was in the parsonage as the church was too small), when a big low-boy truck with a dozer on the back pulled in beside the church. Glenn Starks walked in and said, "Preacher, Elmer sent me over to dig the basement. He said you would show me where to dig." So, I went back and stepped off from the back of the church to extend the basement back a long ways. I pulled a calendar off the wall and drew blueprints upon it from which we built for five years, and the following pastor continued to build.

In short order we had the basement in and closed, as winter was coming on. We had a very large area that we could meet in. As soon as the spring weather broke we built on top, tore out the back wall of the church, and added more pews all the way down. We now had a building four times larger. We added a baptistery; the church was really growing.

I announced to the church that I wanted to have a Sunday School contest. I wanted us to grow to have the largest Sunday School in Dwight, Illinois. They were all in favor of that. I called all of the churches to see what their Sunday School and church attendance was running and was I ever disappointed! We were already the largest Sunday School and church in Dwight, Illinois. This was a Scandinavian town and most of the people were Lutheran, a few Methodist and some Catholic. They really did not know what Baptists were and thought maybe they swung from chandeliers and foamed at the mouth. I hadn't been there long before I started sending out bulk mailings and a monthly newspaper with gospel messages in them, my picture and a picture of the church; the same as I had done in Harrison.

I also found out there was a radio station in Sterling, Illinois, about 40 or 50 miles away. I talked to them and arranged to have a daily radio program. It was the nearest station to Dwight; the station that everyone listened to. Through a phone line I had a microphone and an amplifier that sent my message to the radio station. I broadcast every morning live from my office; the program was called "From the Pastor's Study." They would play the theme song at the station, I would hear it on my radio, turn my radio down and preach for 15 minutes every morning. Then they would play a closing song as it went off. Virtually everyone in our town would hear me preach every morning, and my, did the doors begin to open! People were not afraid as they realized we did not foam at the mouth or swing from chandeliers, and we continued to see souls saved. We even got a couple of buses and went out to surrounding areas and brought young people into church.

Things grew and grew and God blessed in a marvelous way. Young men were called into the ministry and many young ladies went off to either become pastor's wives or Christian school teachers.

After five years my health had continued to deteriorate. Often I had to preach with oxygen on and the song leader would have to sing several stanzas before I could quit coughing. I would virtually lay on the pulpit as I preached. Finally some of the people in my church, along with my wife, took me to Mayo Clinic in Rochester, Minnesota. They told me I had about three months to live unless I went West. I had never been west of the Mississippi, but I had a new station wagon, and my parents came, and with oxygen, and a bed in the back we started driving west. We went to Denver, Colorado, and the closer we got, the better I started feeling. Finally when we got there Dr. Ed Nelson talked to me and said, "If you don't find something, come back here and help me and get back on your feet."

I remember we went to Phoenix and on to Tucson, Arizona. We checked out a couple of churches in Arizona but it just didn't feel right. We came back to Las Cruces, New Mexico, where we were going to turn north on Interstate 25, go to Albuquerque and then head back to Illinois. Looking at the map, I said, "Let's go see Juarez, Mexico," as it was only 50 miles away. So we drove over and saw the worst part of the slums of El Paso, Texas, walked across the bridge into Juarez for a couple of hours, came back, got in our car and went on to Albuquerque. In Albuquerque I met Pastor Bert Singletary and visited with him. Then we headed back to Illinois.

I was feeling well, but it wasn't very long after I got back to Illinois that I started feeling very bad once again. Dr. Ed Nelson asked me to come and be with him. The First Baptist Church in Dwight said, "Leave your family, and go, and we will take care of them. You try to get established, and back on your feet." I took two other people who needed a ride to Denver, dropped them off, and walked into the church.

Dr. Nelson said, "Someone has been trying to reach you from El Paso."

I said, "I can't imagine why, I certainly don't know anyone there." He gave me the number and I called. They said, "We have already bought your airplane ticket. We called you in Dwight and found out from your wife that you were already on your way to Denver. You have an airplane ticket to fly down here on Saturday and preach for us Sunday, April 19th."

Well, I went to the airport and flew down. Two men met me at the airport, Mr. Combs and Mr. Clark. They had asked each other how they would know who I was, but when they saw me get off the plane with a small brimmed hat they said "that has to be him." Everyone else wore cowboy hats (as I now do). They put me in a motel and I preached Sunday morning and Sunday night, then got on the plane and flew back to Denver on Monday. On Wednesday they called and said they had voted unanimously to call me as their pastor.

I got in my car and drove to El Paso. I had brought a small bed that one of our children had slept in, a card table and a folding chair, so I moved into the large parsonage. I would go back and get my wife and family as soon as school was out. I went to the church, found my office, and opened the desk drawer. I found a long series of letters from the vice-president of the bank that had never been opened saying that the church was many thousands of dollars behind in their sinking fund to pay their building payments. The further I went, the larger the amounts got, until finally I got to the end of the letters and they said the bank was going to foreclose on the church. I found the directions to the bank and found the vice-president's office, Mr. Lydiak. I walked in and introduced myself, and he said, "Before you ask anything, I assume you found the letters." I told him I had, and I said that none of them had been opened over a two-year span.

He said "Let me give you some good advice. Just pack your suitcase, back up, and keep going. You had nothing to do with this mess, and it is going to be impossible to pull it out."

I said, "Well Mr. Lydiak, I am now the pastor and consider it my personal debt."

Before I left, I made arrangements to take out a personal loan from the bank. At first he said, "I do not know you, and they probably won't be able to pay you," but I gave him the name and number of my banker back in Illinois, and asked him to call Mr. Shelton. After doing so, he loaned me a good-sized amount and asked what I was going to do with it. I said, "I am going to put it in the offering plate and start paying on these bills."

Well, I did, and the church did not pay me for a few weeks. The deacons said they did not know that the payments had not been made, that it was all news to them. So who knows? Anyway, others started getting a burden and giving.

I wrote to all of the bondholders and told them that I was the new pastor. I apologized to them that they had not been able to cash their bonds nor their interest coupons. I promised each one of them that I would not only pay the interest coupons that were due, but I would continue to pay interest on them until the day they cashed them, something I did not have to do. I told them I had taken out a loan and that there was money available, but asked those who needed the money really badly to cash theirs first, if they were due. I promised the others if they would just wait, they would not lose any interest money. I continued to keep them updated, and within two years we had not only made all the weekly payments of nearly $1250 on the sinking fund, but had paid all the past due. We were not the only church in El Paso that had been on this type of program. A group had come in, built the building and sold the bonds, which we paid off 100 percent on the dollar, (not all churches did).

God blessed the church and it grew and grew, in fact we were the fastest growing church in El Paso. We began with a handful of people and grew until our buildings became full and we built additions on.

As I went out and knocked on doors, I realized that many of the people in the area did not speak any English. At that time, most of the families had a personal maid. Young ladies from the interior of Mexico would come and live with a family and clean house, cook, care for children or whatever needed to be done for ten to twelve dollars a week. Usually they would stay for a year, go home for a month's vacation and then return. I asked the people, "Why don't you bring your maids with you to church?" They said they wouldn't understand anything that was being said.

We had a young couple in the church, Richard and Ada Ward. Richard was an electronic genius and his wife was from Puerto Rico. When they moved to El Paso, she did not know a word of English. She started school in the third grade and sat there and cried, as she did not know what the teacher was saying. It wasn't long until she learned English. I used an office in the back of the church, put a window in it and Richard rigged up a public address system. We got a telephone operator's headset so Ada could hear what I was preaching, and as fast as I went, she translated it into Spanish. We had several rows in the back of the church where we had earphones that they could plug in. So the people started bringing their maids to church with them, and they could hear the gospel and began getting saved. Then we started getting other people in the community, and soon it wasn't practical to have enough earphones. So we got a Spanish pastor and built a Spanish chapel in the church. Our Spanish work grew and grew and many souls were saved.

I had Bill and Mary Rice come for a revival meeting and asked them to teach sign language in the daytime. My wife learned sign language as well. This was after we were already taking busloads of deaf people to Tennessee in the summer. So we started a deaf department. My wife would teach Sunday School to the hearing impaired, and then she would interpret my sermons in the auditorium in a special section we had set aside for the deaf. We had services conducted in English, Spanish and Sign language. The deaf work grew large enough that we really needed a deaf pastor. So we added on another section, then heard of a young deaf pastor, Allen Snare in Pennsylvania, who was single. He came and became our deaf pastor. We had a printing press and print shop, and since he had been a printer by trade, he ran our press along with me.

The church was booming. We had a dynamic youth director and our youth department was really growing. In fact, we would have 200 teenagers that would sit in the front pews in the auditorium. They were constantly out winning souls and serving the Lord.

We also began a ministry to the military at Fort Bliss. We would send buses out to Ft. Bliss, where we would pick up soldiers; we told them if they would come to church we would give them a nice family Sunday dinner. My wife would have 20 to 30 service men each Sunday and Don and Ruth Wakefield would sometimes have that many in their home. The soldiers liked to come on the weekend and hang out around the church just to get off base. Things were really, really booming.

I was teaching in the book of Acts where it says daily the Lord added to the church such as should be saved. I said "Why can't we do that here in El Paso?" El Paso is a predominately Catholic town, but we started out, and every day people would call in and tell my secretary how many people they had led to the Lord. She took colored construction paper and cut out strips, and on each strip she would write the day, the date and the number that had been saved the previous day, add it to the chain, and staple it together. The chain began to grow down the side of the church and we kept stressing the importance of not letting the chain be broken. The chain grew and grew.

It seemed Wednesday was always the most difficult day, I don't know why. But on Wednesday when no on had called in I would ask, in the mid-week services, "Has anyone led someone to the Lord today?" A hush would fall over the church and people would be troubled. They could not wait for church to be over. They would rush out, go to parking lots, parks, door to door; wherever they could find people still up. Wednesday usually turned out to be our largest number of souls won, as no one wanted the chain to be broken.

We baptized every Sunday morning, Sunday night, and Wednesday night. The church continued to grow and we were in building programs adding on. We started a Christian day care and a Christian school, Kindergarten through 12th grade. We had a large lunchroom where we fed 200 students and teachers each day. Yes, things were booming and really growing. It was during this time that I started the Apache Creek Deaf and Youth Ranch, but we will leave that until later. We had built large assembly rooms for the junior department and the teen department, and had areas where they divided up for classes, but the teens we held in large assemblies and there has never been a group of teenagers more on fire for the Lord. The service men were on fire for the Lord and it seemed that things could never be better. I had a Sunday morning program on KHEY radio, one of the main radio stations in El Paso and the gospel was going forth. We had gone from one of the smallest churches in town to one of the largest and God was blessing in a mighty way.

God was blessing, but things began to happen. In fact, they had started prior to this. Priests would follow our buses and tell the children that something would happen to them if they rode our buses to church. Thousands of Catholics were coming to accept Jesus Christ as Savior; some came to our church and some stayed in their own. Finally one Sunday morning when our bus drivers came to drive our six bus routes, they found that none of them had gas although they had been filled with gas on Saturday. After further checking, they found that holes had been punctured in the bottom of the tanks and all of the gasoline had run out. We had these repaired and filled again, and in a couple of weeks when the drivers came to get in the buses they found they could not put them in gear, for all of the gearshifts had been sawed off at the floor level with a hack saw. We had to go to junkyards and get new gearshifts to get them going again.

Also during this time, we found that when people would come out to their cars after church, some of their battery cables had been cut and batteries stolen. This continued on for a period of five years. The church was still growing, but people were upset about all of this happening.

Finally we began to put men out on the parking lot, most of the men of the church, to try and protect our vehicles from the cholos (Mexican gang members).

One large group of cholos would come from one direction, and half of our men would go to chase them off. Another group would then come from another direction, and the other half would chase them off, then a third group would slip in, and when our men would come back all of the windshields of the cars would be smashed. The church was constantly broken into. They would break into my office, steal anything they wanted, turn my desk upside down, dump the drawers out, dump out the filing cabinets, break the pictures that were on the wall, and throw them on the stack. It was absolute chaos. This went on and on. We had to hire an armed guard with a Doberman Pinscher to patrol our school to keep our students safe.

We also came one Sunday morning and they had not only broken out the windows on the buses, but had taken pickup trucks with chains on either side and pulled out all the window posts, and the tops of the buses were laying on the seats. All we could do then was sell them for scrap iron. During this time, when I was building the camp, other things began to happen as well. Six times they tried to assassinate me. One week after Brother Hyles had come to preach at our church, I took him to the airport early Monday morning, came back to the office, started to sit down, and fell across my desk. I was rushed to the hospital and was very ill. We held a large "Sword of the Lord" Conference on Soul Winning and Revival, and I was not even able to attend the meetings.

Dr. Jack Hyles came to our house and prayed for me, and told my wife that he had a very special heart doctor in his church. As soon as he got back, he would have the doctor call us each day to see how I was doing. He said, "I have made arrangements at the airport. On the first day that your husband is able to travel there will be a direct flight to Chicago, and the doctor will be waiting for him." So one day when I felt better, we flew to Chicago and Mr. Olsen met us with a wheelchair at the plane, took us out to a car and on to the hospital. Dr. Jack Hyles furnished a motel for my wife and gave her a car to drive. I got better but I did not get well.

This continued, but after I collapsed and went to the hospital the church members did not expect me to survive, so different pastors were concerned and would have someone else preach in their church and come and preach for me. Things really started going down and the people decided that their pastor was not coming back. Our youth director had left prior to this, so people decided that there were other churches that they could go to where their car would be in one piece when they came out after church.

After about six months when I was finally able to attend church once again, I walked in to preach and there were only 35 people. The rest had fled. My, how sickening! I also found that the associate during that time had not made any of the building fund payments and we were $50,000 in the red. I went to the bank, and as I walked in Mr. Lydick rushed out and threw his arms around me and said, "We thought you were gone and that the church was going to be gone too." I took out a personal loan that day for $50,000 and caught the building fund payments up. I worked for many years to get it paid off. The church ended up being debt free and the entire loan was paid off. But it was really a struggle.

Finally we had to move from the church building on Sundays. We held services in the gymnasium of a school north of the freeway. We did this for quite awhile, but it was difficult. We tried to sell the church but those who had money didn't want a church in that area. Finally we practically gave it to a Spanish church at just a fraction of what the property was worth and moved into a shopping center. We rented five store fronts and made a church, even put white columns out front and a steeple on top, and our church began to grow. Since we had left the Bel Air area of El Paso, we changed our name from Bel Air Baptist Church to Temple Baptist Church.

After being there a few years the church bought an old factory at the edge of town which was a block, solid cement building. It had been a metal works factory that had lost their government contract. It had been sitting empty and was rat infested and full of trash. We made arrangements to buy the property. The church members thought I had absolutely lost my mind and said they didn't ever see how we could have church there. We worked and worked, and during this time I was very ill and began to have mini strokes.

One day while working out at the church, I passed out. There was no electricity in the building and no air conditioning, it was 110 degrees; I knew I had to get out and get help. I thought if I could get in my truck and get to the Circle K store that had been built out in the desert ahead of the city, that they would get help for me. I remember trying to crawl, blacking out, and crawling some more and somehow getting to the truck. The truck was in "grandma gear" and I don't remember anything else. This was about 15 miles from our home. The kids were out playing in the yard when they saw the truck chugging along without my foot on the gas pedal and realized it was me. When I did not stop at the house they ran out, jumped in the truck, shut the key off, stopped the truck and got me in the house.

Finally we got the church remodeled and when we opened for services people came in and their mouths fell open. It was one of the most beautiful auditoriums they had ever seen. We had built big white columns to cover the steel beams where cranes had previously hung. We added a baptistry in the front and bought pews from another church that had closed in the same area where our church had had so many problems. It was a beautiful church and once again it began to grow and rebuild in spite of my poor health.

Finally when I got completely down, another group came in to help me. Then when I started getting better and was out of town, they announced that they were moving and starting a new church, and they took 400 of our members.

I say this only because I want you to know that God is a God of Heaven and through faith He can still do anything for those who believe Him even though it looks like everything is over. It was far from over.

Before I leave this, let me back up and tell you of something marvelous that happened. After five years of the situation with the cholos, and we had moved out

Vision, Adventure, Faith

of the area, I was at ACE Christian School convention in Midland, Texas. After one of the services a man came to me that I had never seen before, and said he wanted to apologize. I looked at the man, puzzled, and said, "I can't imagine why you would want to apologize to me. I have never seen you before."

He said, "That's right, you have not seen me but when I tell you some things, you will know who I am." I had always thought someone was behind all of the cholos and all of the troubles that we had had. Many attempts had been made on my life but each had failed. The man told me that he was the one behind all of the cholos that attacked me, all of the six assassination attempts on my life. He said, "I was a Jesuit priest, and it was my job to drive you out or to kill you. But when it went on year after year and you refused to quit and you refused to leave, I got to the point that I could not sleep at night."

He told me of each of the assassination attempts, of how they had planned and organized all of the attacks on the church, how they had driven away most of our people. "But it did not bring peace," he said. "I became so troubled and could not understand why you would not quit and why we could not kill you. One day as I sat on a park bench, a couple of charismatic Christians came by and led me to the Lord. I am now starting a charismatic church over on the other side of El Paso, but I have to get your forgiveness for all that I have done to you." I told him that he was forgiven and I was glad that I finally knew what was behind all of it. Yes, even through great trials and tribulations God is working.

40

God has blessed Mrs. Lang and I with nine wonderful children. Heather was born July 14th , 1958, while we lived in Paris, Illinois. She and her husband, two sons, daughter and two grandchildren live in Houston, Texas. Glenda was born in Shephardsville, Indiana, on June 25th, 1959, and lives with her husband and son in El Paso, Texas. Alisa was born while we lived in Harrison, Illinois on May 15th, 1961, and lives in Garland, Texas, with her husband, daughter and son. Kevin was born on November 14th, 1962, also in Harrison and now lives in Orlando, Florida with his wife and four sons. Brian was born February 9th, 1964, also in Harrison, and I delivered him at home. He now lives in Orlando, Florida with his wife, twin sons, and three grandchildren. Troy was born December 8th, 1965, in Dwight, Illinois; I also delivered him at home. Now he lives in Chaparral, New Mexico, (next to El Paso) with his wife. Kent was born September 27th, 1968, in Dwight, and I also delivered him at home. He now lives here at the ranch next to us. Brent was also born in Dwight, IL, on October 7th, 1969. He was a hotel engineer in Orlando, Florida and went to be with the Lord when he accidentally fell 11 floors 2 weeks after his 24th birthday. We miss him very much! Craig was born January 26th, 1979, in El Paso, Texas. He now lives here at the Ranch with his wife, two daughters, and a son. He is co-pastor of our church and director of the Apache Creek Deaf and Youth Ranch. He is also the vice president of our board, and will step up into my place when I am gone. I wanted to mention each one of them because they sacrificed right along with us and worked with us through these many years. THANK

YOU TO EACH AND EVERY ONE OF YOU. We are so proud of each of you and thankful you are godly men and woman today!

Chapter 2

A Vision For the Deaf

I had never given deafness a thought, had never known anyone who was deaf, and was busy working building a church in Dwight, Illinois, where I was pastor of the First Baptist Church. I had invited Bill Rice III for a two-week revival meeting for the second time. The first time he was single, but this time he had just married Mary. When they arrived on Sunday, she said to me, "If you have any deaf here, I will be glad to interpret for them. Well, I had no idea if there were any deaf in Dwight, but I told her if there were any, I would see if I could have them there on Monday evening.

I scoured the town and found that there was a Methodist family who had a teenage deaf daughter who I believe was 16 at the time, and she happened to be home from deaf school. I told them all about the revival meeting, that it would be held for the next two weeks, and that our services would be interpreted for the deaf. They became very excited and said certainly they would come to the Baptist church if their daughter could hear and understand the Bible. They said, "When she is home, she always goes to church with us, but of course she has no idea of what is going on. She just sits quietly and looks around until the service is over, and then leaves with us."

On Monday night, sure enough, they were there, in fact they were there for every service throughout the revival meeting. Mary had been interpreting for this young lady for three or four days and I asked Mary and the young lady if I could talk to them. They came to my office, and through Mary I asked the young lady if she knew Jesus Christ. A very puzzled look came over her face and she thought and thought, and then she signed back, "I know He does not go to our deaf school because if He did, I would know Him. He probably lives here in Dwight, Illinois, but you see I can't talk to people here so I have never met Him." It broke my heart. I have had that happen all over the country when I have asked deaf people the same question.

I remember many years later talking to a deaf couple in Colorado Springs, Colorado, who were in their seventies, and asking if they knew Jesus Christ. Again, they talked back and forth in sign language and finally said, "Well, we know He doesn't belong to our deaf club or we would know Him, but you see we can't talk to the other people. I am sure He lives here in Colorado Springs, but, no we do not know Him." You see, most people don't understand all that is involved in deafness. Deaf people are not dumb, though they used to say "deaf and dumb," the "dumb" meant they were not able to speak. Deaf people are just as intelligent and in many ways sharper than other people, because they have to use their eyes so keenly. You can give them a gospel tract about Jesus but it means absolutely nothing to them as they have no idea who He is. You can talk to them about Heaven, but they have no conception of that.

Many times when deaf people come to our camp, they receive Jesus Christ as their Savior. We always start teaching with creation, then sin, God sending His Son, the baby Jesus. Often their eyes will light up and they will say, "That is the baby in the manger at Christmastime?" They would have no idea.

We have had many come to camp over the years, and we ask them how many are in their family, and they will sign to us maybe a couple of brothers and sisters. When we ask what their names are, many have responded, "I don't know." They have a sign name for them, but they say, "No one has ever told us their name." How sad! Many times parents don't even know how to talk to their deaf children so they send them off to deaf schools. During the summer when they are home, they point at things and get by the best they can.

Anyway, back to the young girl. She did not know who Jesus Christ was, and I had received a burden and vision for the deaf. She continued to learn through the revival meeting and before it was over she knew who Jesus Christ was because she had accepted Him as her Lord and Savior and He lived in her heart. Oh how thrilled she was! She went back to deaf school but, I never got away from that burden about the deaf. It is perhaps one of the greatest mission fields in the world today. The Bible says in Isaiah 29:18 "In that day the deaf shall hear the words of the book."

Most deaf works in the world today started because Dr. and Mrs. Bill Rice had a little girl. He was going to Moody Bible Institute in Chicago and would shovel snow in the winter and do odd jobs to put himself through school. They lived in a damp basement apartment and when their oldest daughter, Betty, got sick, they were concerned but very poor. They took her to a doctor who looked at her and said she would be fine. But during the night she got worse with a very high fever and they called the doctor. He said, "Give her an aspirin and she will be fine." By the next day she was extremely ill and they had to take her to a clinic, but it was too late. The high fever had destroyed her eardrums.

Most deaf people either lose their hearing through a high fever such as those that come with spinal meningitis, or their mothers had German measles while they were being carried.

While in Dwight, each summer I would drive with a busload of our young people to Murfreesboro, Tennessee to see Dr. Bill and Cathy Rice. They had been friends down through the years; I knew Bill III and the other children when they were little. That burden about the deaf never left me.

In 1970 when we moved to El Paso, Texas, because of my health, I was soon going to see a great need for reaching the deaf.

Chapter 3

The Vision, the Need, and the Opportunity

When we moved to El Paso, Texas, I found that there were a lot of deaf people. In fact, there were hundreds all over the city. I found that there was one church that had a deaf couple in it and their daughter interpreted for them, but that was pretty much the deaf work. I could not find any deaf camps throughout the West. As I ran into more and more deaf, though at the time my wife and I did not know how to sign to them, I became burdened. I went to the Lion's Club, because they have camps for handicapped children, and asked them if I could get a bus load of deaf, would they charter the bus so that I could take the kids to a deaf camp in Tennessee at the Bill Rice Ranch. Since it was a year in advance they said they would be glad to do that.

Throughout the year I called and they said, "Yes, you get them ready and we will provide the bus and driver." My wife and I had found deaf people, and through them found others. Though we had to write notes everywhere we went and often had to take someone who spoke Spanish with us as usually their parents did not know English, we began to gather up a group of deaf. We were going to leave on a Saturday morning to take them to camp and had everything all set to go.

On the Monday before the Saturday, we got a call from someone at the Lion's Club, who said, "We are sorry, but we will not be able to charter a bus for you. It is just too expensive." Well, this would be a time I guess we could say, "Sorry, we can't go." But I have never turned back; if the door is closed I try to find a window that I can go through. I began searching desperately for some way to get the deaf there. To charter the bus was way beyond our means, so I kept praying Lord open a door for us to take these deaf children to camp. It was late Friday afternoon and I was going down Alameda Street in El Paso and praying, "Lord, please show me how we are going to get the deaf to camp in the morning." They were to be at the church at 9:00 a.m. and I still had no idea how we were going to get them to Tennessee. As I drove by Bowen Trailer Park I noticed an old Greyhound bus sitting there. I went in and inquired of Mr. Bowen and he said it was a 1952 model Greyhound (this was in 1972). So I asked him how much he would charge to rent me the bus and told him what I had in mind. He said, "I will rent you the bus for $2000."

I said, "I want to rent it not buy it."

He said, "I am sorry but that is the price." I asked him how much he wanted to sell the bus for and he said he would sell the bus for $4,000. I told him that his bus was sold, but the bank was closed and I could not get a loan. I told him about all of the deaf that would be at the church at 9:00 a.m. for the trip to Tennessee. I said, "If you will let me take the bus now, when I get back a week from Monday I will go to the bank and take out a $4000 loan and pay you for the bus."

He said, "Pastor Lang, you have a good reputation here in El Paso," and he shook hands on the deal.

I parked my car, got in the bus and drove off. I had never driven a Greyhound before, though I had driven school buses. I drove it back, and contacted a man in our church that had a tire store; the tires on the front were really bad. I made arrangements to meet him at his tire store at 7:00 a.m. the next morning to get two new tires put on the front of the bus. I got it all fueled up and ready to go and was back at the church by 9:00. The deaf were all there and piled onto the bus. We loaded up a big garbage can full of ice and all kinds of sodas and sandwiches, cookies, chips, etc. and took off for Tennessee some 1500 miles east. We had driven all day and most of the night and were going through Nashville, when suddenly there was a funny noise back in the engine compartment. The bus died and I coasted off of the upcoming ramp. We coasted as far as we could and I prayed and asked the Lord to send us help. I looked up and there was an old black man knocking on the door. I opened the door and he said, "Sirs, you ought not to be in this part of town. It might not be safe for you."

I said, "Well I am sorry but my bus won't run and I can't go anywhere." He was such a kind gentleman; I asked him if he knew a diesel mechanic and a shop.

He said, "Yassah, I do. It is right around the corner." He went and got the mechanic out of bed, who came with a truck and towed our bus into his shop at about 3:00am. The deaf kids had been riding a long time. We could only write notes back and forth to them, and they wanted to get off the bus. So the first thing we knew they were running up and down the streets and the poor black man was so nervous for them. I called Dr. Cathy Rice, woke her up, told her our situation and asked if she could send a bus to pick up our deaf. She so graciously did, and after about an hour an old school bus pulled up. The driver's name was Lee Robertson; later Lee and his family came and worked for us at the Ranch in Apache Creek on two different occasions.

We loaded up and went to camp and were there all week. The mechanic discovered that the blower had gone out on the engine and said it would take him a good part of the week to get the part and get it fixed. My, how God worked in the hearts of these young deaf people! All of them were of Spanish descent and none of them had any idea who Jesus Christ was, but by the time the week was over, all had not only learned who He was but had accepted Him as their Lord and Savior. What a difference there was in their lives! Many of those that were saved in that busload we saw later come into our church and help our deaf department to grow.

Chapter 4

Looking for Land

This is where the vision and faith really comes into being. I continued taking the deaf to Tennessee for the next few years. I kept asking Dr. Bill if he would come west and start a camp. He always turned me down. I would talk to him not only when I would see him, but I also wrote him. One day I got an answer to a letter that I had written that really caught me off guard. In it he said, "I don't want you to ever write me again about starting a camp in the West. I have all I can handle here and I am not interested in coming west and starting another camp. Furthermore, God did not give me the burden to start a camp in the West, he has given you the burden so get busy and do it."

Well, I was set back by that. I began to pray about it, and in early 1975 after I had been talking about it, praying about and talking to the church about it, I decided to set off and look for land. Of course I had no idea what I was getting into. A couple in the church loaned me a nice pickup truck that had a camper on the back with a place where I could sleep and eat. I had business in Farmington, New Mexico. I decided I would probably come back around Silver City somewhere and look for land to build the camp. Now in 1975, road maps were not all they were talked up to be; in fact, even today they are not. For example, the road that goes between my house and my son's house is Route 49. You had better have a four-wheel drive vehicle if you are going up that dirt road, as it is very steep and very difficult, with lots of gates to open. Well, that is the way most of the roads were in western New Mexico. The only paved road in western United States that went from the bottom of the state to the top was I-25; between there and the Arizona border is 150 miles.

I had gone to Albuquerque and angled across to Farmington and in checking my map, sure enough, it showed a road that went straight down the back side of New Mexico to Silver City, so I got on that road and I traveled. It was paved all the way to Gallup. From Gallup on, things began to change. The gravel road turned into dirt trails. It was in the spring of the year, and things were freezing and thawing and I kept getting stuck.

Finally, I made my way on down and came to a place named Fence Lake. I was nearly out of gas and I was so thrilled to see that they had a gas pump. There was about a foot of water standing around the tanks and a bunch of old cars parked around them so I stopped and went in the store and asked them if they could move the cars so I could pull up and fill my truck up with gas. They informed me that they only sold gas during the summer months so I would not be able to buy any gas. I said, "Well fine, just put another plate on the table because I will be your house guest until summer comes." Well, they looked at one another and decided maybe they could move some of the cars and pump me some gas, and they did.

The roads worsened, and down the road awhile the fuel pump went out on the truck. There I sat. Well, there was only one thing to do. I had come a long way and I knew there were no parts store back where I had gotten gas, so I decided to walk south where the map showed there was a place called Quemado. I walked and walked and walked, and finally came to Quemado exhausted. I came to a station and told them I needed a fuel pump. Of course they did not have fuel pump for the Ford truck, but they did have an electric fuel pump which I bought. I asked if there was any way they could take me back to where my truck was. They shook their heads "no" as they weren't going to try to go down that mud road; besides, they could not be away from the station. So I walked and walked and I walked some more and finally got back to the truck totally exhausted. I took off my muddy clothes and went to bed in the camper.

The next morning I managed to mount the electric fuel pump, hook it to the battery and get the truck started. After many attempts and each time getting stuck, I finally got to Quemado, but the roads south of Quemado were no better. You simply drove through the trees on sort of a deer trail, and when you got stuck you did your best to jack it up, put something under the wheels and go a little further. I had spent a couple of days doing this in the mud when all of a sudden I came to a brand new road in the middle of nowhere. I thought to myself, "What is this road doing here?" I mean it just stopped among the pine trees. I managed to get up on the road and said to myself, "I am getting as far from this God-forsaken country as I can."

Well the road went down a very steep grade into what had been a box canyon. When I got to the bottom of the box canyon, the Lord spoke to my heart in a very definite way. I stopped the truck and got out and walked out onto this property. It was all grown up in weeds and I said, "Lord, are you trying to tell me something?" I was sure He was, but I wanted something to prove it. I had no idea what lay ahead on the road but decided to proceed on until the Lord showed me something definite.

About six miles down I came to a T in the road, and there was an old country Apache Creek store with gas pumps. I pulled up to the pump as I was getting low on gas again and an older man came out to pump the gas. His name was Preston Porter. I believe that God had put Preston there just for me. He was up in years; he did not work at the station but just hung out there a lot and pumped gas for something to do. Often the owners would go off, as they had on this occasion, and leave him to run the store. He was not paid, he just enjoyed doing it. After we filled the truck with gas and I paid him for it, I asked, "Mr. Porter, do you know of any land for sale around here?"

He said, "Oh no, it is almost impossible to find land to buy here." Most of the land was U.S. Forest Land

and what little private land there was along the streams usually no one wanted to sell. Often a rancher might have 40 acres of deeded land and maybe lease 100 sections of Forest land. One section is a mile square and 640 acres. A rancher may have 100 square miles (64,000 acres) of U.S. Forest land, that they would run their cattle on, but it was very difficult to buy private land. I told Mr. Porter what my burden was, that I wanted to build a camp where I could bring deaf children, where I could bring poor children, where I could bring Indian children, where I could bring church groups and tell them about the Lord Jesus Christ.

As I talked to Mr. Porter, tears began to run down his cheeks and he said, "Oh wouldn't that be wonderful." He then gave me his testimony. He said, "I have always been a member of the Presbyterian Church here, but that is not where I got saved. When I was a young man there was a young prize fighter that used to come to Reserve, which was twelve miles from the store, and set up a boxing ring. He was a little short man with very broad shoulders. He said he would pay anyone 50 cents if they could get in the ring and knock him out and win the rounds. He didn't give away many 50 cent pieces. After he had fought everyone who cared to challenge him and a big crowd had come, then he would pull out his Bible and he would preach." I asked him what that prizefighter's name was, and he said his name was Eschol Cosby. I knew Eschol Cosby very well; he had been in our church in El Paso many times. He had a singing group made up of him, his wife, his son and daughter-in-law, and a daughter.

I said, "I know Eschol Cosby."

He said, "Well, it was after one of those boxing matches when he preached that I took Jesus Christ into my heart as my Lord and Savior. Not only I, but my brother did as well. Over the years I have never forgotten that. In this community every so often when a boy or girl becomes about 12 or 13 years old, I will tell their parents 'I need to go to Springerville, Arizona, 85 miles away to the nearest supermarket and drugstore, to get groceries, and I wonder if your son or daughter could go with me.'" He said, "On Sunday morning, I would hurry over there, to the First Baptist Church, where they specialized in telling people how to get saved. I have seen many of the young people here in this community get saved that way. Wouldn't it be wonderful if this could happen here?"

Then he said, "You know, I know the perfect place. This canyon used to be an old robber's roost. Many outlaws lived here as the box canyon ended at a big waterfall at the other end and it was very difficult to get in or out other than here by the store. So there were lots of outlaw gangs. In fact, the one who owned the ranch that you might buy had been a train robber and when he died, I understand that many people went onto the ranch and did a lot of digging. Whether they ever found the gold that he had robbed from trains or not, I don't know. He left the land to his nephew. At the ranch just north of us there was a three room log cabin that just burned a few years ago. At one time that cabin had 32 rooms and it ran up along the creek. Thirty-two outlaw families lived there, part of the Butch Cassidy gang. Billy the Kid used to ride up the canyon and would stop at the Milligan's, just before our ranch, and Grandma Milligan would say, 'Billy, take the fiddle from the wall and play a tune for me and I will fix you some vittles,' and he would play away as she fried some potatoes and dipped up some beans off the back of the stove for him. Yes, it had quite a history of outlaws. Fact is, up on the north end of the ranch is Whiskey Creek. You can imagine what they used to make in stills up that creek; we have found the ruins of some of them. "Anyway," he said, "wouldn't it be wonderful if this old robber's roost could be a place where people could come and know Jesus Christ as their Savior?"

He said, There is a ranch that a man inherited, though he has never lived on it. He comes out here for vacation each summer and everyone has tried to buy the land but he won't sell it." He said he knew it was just the place and he gave me directions.

When I went back, it was the same place that the Lord had spoken to my heart about, where I had knelt and prayed and asked God for a sign. I said, "Lord if this is the land for us, You will have to make it possible." I went back and said, "Mr. Porter, do you have the name and phone number of this man?" He said, "Yes, it is owned by J. C. and Martha Tucker and I believe somewhere in the store there might be phone number for them. He went and looked and looked and finally found the phone number. He told me that he was a retired jeweler who lived in Santa Fe, New Mexico. Although, this was the year they started the phone company in that part of New Mexico, 1975, there still were no phones available, so I had to drive 125 miles to Silver City before I found a pay phone and was able to call Mr. Tucker. I told him who I was, that I had been to his land and that I would like to buy it for a youth camp. He said, "The land is not for sale," and hung up. Still, I knew that God had said this was the place. I continued to work to take deaf children back to Tennessee that summer. In fact, I was not only taking busloads in our bus that we had bought in El Paso, but I was also trying to get others to do the same. I made a trip to the deaf school in Santa Fe to convince them to go. Though we could not take them with us from El Paso we told them we would see if maybe we could find someone from Colorado Springs to take them. While I was there, I called Mr. Tucker again. He said, "I told you the land is not for sale."

I went on to Colorado Springs and visited the deaf and blind school there and once again tried to get a church in the area to take them to Tennessee. I had a special meeting for the deaf at the Cornerstone Baptist Church with Pastor Dean Miller. From there we went on to a deaf school in Denver, which was a local school for the Denver people, and tried to find someone there that perhaps would take the deaf to camp. When I came back to Santa Fe I got a phone book and looked for Mr. Tucker's address. I found it and made some inquiries and found his home. When I got to the home there was a sign out front that said, "Watch Repairs." He was a retired jeweler from Las Cruces, New Mexico, who had retired in Santa Fe. His uncle, John Tucker, had died in the old cabin on the ranch (where our youngest son Craig and his family now live). It is interesting to read about the old timers who would die in their cabins and often wouldn't be found for some time. Ben Lilly said he never found a dog that was with his master that did anything but protect the body, but if the man had cats, the cats would eat the body. Interesting, isn't it?

Anyway, as I saw the sign, I took my wristwatch off and walked up to the door holding it in my hand. He looked up, told me to come in and have a seat and he would get with me in a little while. He finished working on the watch that he was working with and came over and said, "Now, let me see your watch young man."

I said, "Oh there is nothing wrong with my watch, I was just holding it." I began to talk to him about his property and for two hours I told him and his wife of my burden, my vision for helping deaf children, inner city children, Indian children, mountain children, church children, etc.

After two hours tears were trickling down their cheeks and he looked at me and said, "Oh, I am so selfish. My wife and I spend two weeks there at the ranch each summer looking for agate, crystals and all of the rocks which are in abundance. Other than that we never go there. Everybody has tried to buy it but we just enjoyed having the place that we inherited to be able to visit in the summer, and the taxes are cheap. However, I think you have a far greater need of it than we do."

We discussed the price, which seemed like an awful lot of money then, $330 an acre. He said that he would sell it to us and finance it for ten years at 7 ½ percent interest and carry the note himself. He asked how much I could put down. I knew what I had in my wallet as I had just filled my Volkswagen with gas and knew it would get me back to El Paso. I said, "I have five dollars left in my wallet that I can give you today as a down-payment."

He sort of got a frown on his face and said, "I was thinking more like $30,000 down."

I said, "Mr. Tucker, if you will shake hands on the $5 I have today, by the end of the year I will raise the $30,000 down-payment. In the meantime, I would like to use the property just for the kids in my church." We had 200 teenagers, we had lots of junior and junior high boys and girls, and we could pretty well keep it busy through the summer.

He thought about it for a while, stood up, put out his hand, and said, "I will take the five dollars and shake on it." I gave him the five dollars and we shook on the deal.

Where was I going to get $30,000 to put down? Well, I wasn't bothered about that. God had said this was the place, God would make a way! How important Hebrews 11:6 is, as well as other scriptures throughout the Bible when it comes to faith.

For without faith it is impossible to please Him, for we must believe that He IS, and that He is a rewarder of them that diligently seek Him.

(Hebrews 11:6)

I am a firm believer that regardless of what it might be, if God is in it, there is absolutely nothing too big or too hard for God. I think all along the path God wants us to keep that faith and that dependence upon Him. Have you ever thought about the little word IS? If God IS and He IS, then He is the creator of all of Heaven and Earth. He is the creator of everything on Earth, He is the creator of mankind, He holds everything in His hand. Not only did He make everything, but by Him all things consist. The problem is so many times we fret and stew and worry which is a good indication that we are not convinced that He IS.

So, I shook hands and left. We were going to use the land all summer, but we could not build on it until we had put down the down-payment. I did ask permission to cut some dead trees, and he said that would be fine. We could use them to sit on or whatever.

I went back home and announced that we had purchased the Ranch. The church did not take responsibility for it; I was totally responsible for raising funds, but many people in the church did as I did and borrowed money. I borrowed as much as I could get, many others borrowed $500 and donated it. This was still just a drop in the bucket of the $30,000 we needed to raise by the end of the year.

All summer long, week after week, our 1952 model Greyhound bus made trips back and forth to the ranch taking kids. There was an old two-room cabin on the ranch that had a lean-to on the back that was rat infested. We cleaned it out, shooed out the rats, and set up as a snack shop selling pop and candy out the side door. The two rooms of the house, with the bathroom off the back (that the Tuckers had added to use when they were there during the summer), were where the girls slept. They filled all the floor space and usually there was one sleeping in the bathtub. I had bought some tents which I set up under a big elm tree and the boys slept in these tents. All was fine until a big gully washer of rain came one night, when we found our tents were in the path of the run-off from the mountains and our tents were filled with water. Of course, there was no dry place to get in to unless we went and sat in the bus. The next morning we dried out the tents and our sleeping bags and continued on with camps.

My, those were exciting camps that summer! Each week I preached to a different group from our church and often they brought unsaved young people with them who got saved. It was a very exciting time. The place was over grown with weeds, so for the junior boys and girls one of the activities that we would have in junior weeks was a Sadie Hawkins's Day race. If you ever read Lil' Abner, you know what I am talking about. I thought that if there is anything a young boy that age doesn't want is to have anything to do with girls. So I announced we were going to have Sadie Hawkins's Day races and we would give the boys a head start. If the girls caught them, the boy had to buy the girl a candy bar. Well, this upped our snack shop business and all of that racing sure tromped down the weeds around the ranch. Poor momma's, when the kids came home, their clothes, socks and shirts all were so imbedded with stick tight weeds and burrs that most of them just burned the clothes instead of trying to do something with them. Those girls sure could run fast; we sold a lot of candy bars.

We would have services around the bonfire at night and under the tree in the daytime. If it was raining, we would have them sit on our old Greyhound and preach to them there. We had tremendous camps all summer long. For the older kids we had tree cutting contests. We would find two dead trees and get two axes and divide the boys into two teams and the girls, also divided into teams, would stand back and cheer for their group of woodcutters. My, would those boys swing those axes trying to cut those big old dead Ponderosa pines down! Of course I had a bullhorn and cheered them on. They would get blisters on their hands, but they would keep chopping away and then pass it on to the next guy until finally the first tree would fall. The others were determined they could cut their tree down and kept on swinging until it fell. We used these logs for various purposes.

Then I got the idea of preaching contests. I would put one boy up on Goat Mountain in back of the camp, another across the road on Cross Mountain, another down the way up in a tree and we would stand in the valley between the three to see which one we could hear the clearest. My, did they develop lungs! Many of them are pastors today and still preaching. It was a fantastic summer. We sang Bill Harvey's song "I Want That Mountain" every week and added many verses to it as we looked at the mountains and prayed that God would give us this property and help us to raise the down-payment. We sang verses like "I want that mountain, where the grass is always green and the rattlesnakes are mean." There were lots of rattlesnakes in those mountains in those days but after tens of thousands of kids have come over the last 30 years they are harder to find.

One summer I had a rattlesnake that we caught during Indian camp. I put him in an aquarium and set him on the communion table. As they looked on with big eyes, I preached on "The serpent; Satan, is out to get you." I remember the first time I did that we found a mouse and dropped it in there. While I was preaching "the devil is a serpent out to get you," that snake opened his mouth and began swallowing the mouse. Boy, did their eyes get big! They have never forgotten that sermon.

Our young people would hold all-night prayer meetings on Friday nights at church, and would pray and pray that God would give us those mountains and that campground. It took everything that we had. My wife and I have raised nine children and had eight at that time. The money that I had put aside for college and savings went into the fund to make the down-payment. I borrowed all I could borrow, but we still had a lot of money to raise. I bought mailing lists and we began to send out letters to sell Bibles. Anybody that would send $100 I would send them a family Bible. Others would send $10, $15, $20, $35. We sent out hundreds of thousands of letters, as many as 50,000 letters at a time, usually a four- page letter on 8 ½ by 11 paper. Allen Snare, who was our deaf pastor at the church, would start at midnight on Sunday, running the press. I would run it at night and Allen would run it in the daytime. Of course, most of the day I was out knocking on doors and doing church work, but we kept the press going until midnight on Saturday night and then shut it down for Sunday. We printed the letters and folded them, put them in envelopes with a return envelope, and we mailed them to mailing lists all over the country. Maybe one or less percent would send money back, and we sent out many, many Bibles but slowly, slowly we began to raise the money. After we had put together everything we had, by December we were able to make the $30,000 down-payment.

Well, if we thought the struggle was over, we were sure in for a surprise. We were to pay $10,000 a year plus interest. By the time the next year had come around I had become very ill-as I mentioned in the first chapter I had fallen across my desk with a heart attack and was in a hospital in Chicago, Illinois, where a heart doctor in Dr. Hyles's church was caring for me. I was in an oxygen tent and very weak. Elmer Riber, who had been in my church in Dwight, Illinois, 90 miles from Chicago, came to the hospital to see me, hearing I was very ill. He came and asked the nurses if he could see me. The nurse said, "I am sorry, no one but immediate family is allowed in to see him."

Elmer said to the nurse, "If you will let me see him for two minutes I promise you he will feel better." I can remember gasping for air in the oxygen tent. When Elmer walked into the room I was so happy to see him but had difficulty talking. He said, "Pastor, don't try to talk other than to just answer my question if you can. Have you raised the money for the ranch payment?" which was about due.

I shook my head and said, "No, Elmer, it is $19,000

and we have only raised $10,500." He took out his checkbook and wrote a check for $8,500.

He said, "What do I do with the check?" I told him send the check to Barbara Bennett, my secretary at the church and ask her to make the ranch payment. He did after he left, and I did feel better. My, don't we have a wonderful and gracious God when we believe that HE IS!

On another occasion, a Christian man who worked at raising money told me that if I would pay him, I think it was $500, he could raise the money for me easily. I paid him the money, he wrote the letter which we printed and mailed out. The payment that year was $17,000. Nothing came in. I even had to make up the money for the $500 we had paid for the man to write the letter and for the mailing list that we had gotten from him. It looked like all was lost and I was convinced that I had trusted man instead of trusting God. I remember praying and asking God to forgive me and telling Him that I would never again trust man but only trust Him.

The day the payment was due it had not come in. Mrs. Bennett had left work very sad as we had prayed that day that God would make the payment but it had not come in. I mean, we didn't have anything. Barbara Bennett was married to Charlie, a wonderful man. Charlie was so tight with money he could squeeze a nickel until the Indian rode the buffalo, but he was good to his wife. On many, many occasions I had gone to his home and tried to witness to Charlie. He would always say, "You know you don't do that with me," and he would get up, get in his truck and leave. Charlie was a very, very good man. He never cussed, never chewed or smoked, never took part in vices, he was a good man and he couldn't understand why he, who lived a good life, should become a Christian like people he often saw who did not live as good a life as he did. I am still praying for Charlie, I hope he is still alive and I pray that perhaps he has gotten saved somewhere along the line.

Anyway, I was working late in the office and Charlie came strolling in. Charlie said, "Preacher, did you get that ranch payment made?"

I shook my head sadly and said, "No, Charlie we haven't."

He said, "How much do you need?"

I said, "$17,000." I knew that Charlie was very thrifty with his money and wondered why he was asking these questions. He took out his checkbook and wrote out a check for $17,000.

He said, "Preacher this is not a gift, it is a loan and I have no idea how in the world you are ever going to pay me back." He left the office. I remember picking up the phone and calling Barbara.

I said, "Barbara, did you know that Charlie was coming to the office to see me?"

"Well, of course not."

I said, "Barbara, I have a check in my hand, a loan from Charlie that he came and handed me for $17,000."

She said, "Preacher, I don't think that joke is very funny. You and I both know how Charlie won't have anything to do with getting saved and he is so thrifty he would never do such a thing." I had a great deal of difficulty in convincing her that Charlie had really done that. I made a copy of the check that she could look at. The next morning I was at the bank and had the payment on its way. She still would hardly believe it, even seeing the copy of the check and the check that I had written to pay the ranch payment.

It seemed that every year it was such a struggle to make the ranch payments, but each year in some way God worked. I remember one year that it came up to the time and we were short $5,025. We prayed and prayed and gave all that we had, but we were short five thousand and twenty-five dollars. The phone rang and a voice I had never heard before, sort of a gruff voice, said, "This is Ben. I am a backslidden truck driver. God has told me I need to catch up on my tithes. I have heard about your ranch and God told me that is where I ought to send it. Do you have a truck stop in town?"

I said, "Yes."

"What's the name?" I told him and he said, "You be down there in about 20 minutes as I am going to send some back tithes to help you with the camp. He did not know it was the day that the ranch payment was due, how much it was and I did not tell him or anything else. I went to the truck stop praying that God was going to meet this payment, but not expecting to get it paid at the truck stop. I thought maybe $25 or $30, which I would be most grateful for.

I was praying, "Lord, You know we need $5,025."

When I got to the truck stop, gave the code name and told her who I was, she said, "Do you know how much this is?"

And I said, "No, ma'am." It was $5,025. Oh, how I thanked the Lord! This man was a big, big supporter of the ranch for years after that.

Another year we were short $1,750. My home church, the Horace Baptist Church, had taken a special Thanksgiving offering and we got it just when we needed it for the ranch payment. It was $1,750. God always kept track of where we were.

Finally we came to the very last payment. We had worked so hard but we were short an even $5,000. We just could not scrape the money together. During this time, as I mentioned earlier, the church had gone through five years of terrible embattlements. Fact is, during most of these times we had suffered from the embattlement we were going through. The payment was due and I didn't know what we were going to do, but I knew that HE IS so I was praying to the Lord and telling him, "Lord, it certainly will be interesting to see how You make this payment." During the day I got a telephone call. I had never heard the voice before and I have never heard the voice since. He asked, "Where does Apache Creek Deaf and Youth Ranch bank?" I told him. He asked what our account number was. I told him, and I thought, "Well, now he will probably tell me why he is being so nosey and needing to know this," but I heard a click on the other end of the phone. I thought and thought about it and then I called the bank. I was always very good friends with the president and vice-president of the bank. I called and said, "If someone should make a deposit by wire to the Apache Creek account today would you please call me back?"

They said, "We sure will." At 4:55pm I got a call. Someone said, "We just received a wire transfer of $5000 to your account."

I said, "I cannot be there at five o'clock when you lock the doors. But I am leaving the church right now and I will be there in about 10 or 15 minutes. Please be standing at the door to unlock it and let me in when I get there." I rushed to the bank, and when I got there, sure enough the president was standing there at the door. He let me in.

He said, "Pastor, what is so important that you had to get into the bank after hours?"

I said, "Mr. Lydiak, you know our ranch payment is due today and I like paying our bills on time," and I wrote him a check for the final balance. We had paid the Tucker's off a couple of years earlier through a loan from the bank and so this final payment went to the bank. Don't we have a wonderful and a gracious God? Oh, there is a devil out there as a roaring lion going about seeking whom he may devour, but we have a God WHO IS and who answers prayers. More about the ranch in the next chapter.

Chapter 5

Taking My Family to See the Ranch

Before I go on about the actual building of the ranch there is a story that I must tell you about taking my family to see the ranch. I had made arrangements with Mr. Tucker, given him the five dollars and shaken hands, and was planning on a summer of camps for the kids in our church. My wife and eight children (this was before Craig was born) were so excited and wanted to see the ranch, so we decided we would make a trip. School was out except for a high school graduation that was going to be taking place in a couple of days, but one of the young men of the church wanted to go with us, so there were eleven of us in our station wagon.

I decided I wanted to find a shorter route to get to the ranch. You would think I would have learned my lesson by now but I looked at the map and from Truth or Consequences, New Mexico, there was a road that cut catty-cornered across and came out at Apache Creek, New Mexico. I thought, "Goodness, that will cut a lot of miles off the trip." From Reserve, New

Mexico, to Socorro, New Mexico, down to Las Cruces, New Mexico, over across to Deming, up to Silver City and back up to Reserve is an area approximately 125 miles on all sides. Now I know there is not a paved road through that area and so you have to drive around, but I was not so smart yet at that time.

So we left early in the morning and turned off on to this road when we got to Truth or Consequences where the Rio Grande is dammed up and Elephant Butte and Caballo Lake are located. We headed down this road and it was even blacktop for a short distance, then it became a gravel road and there was a sign, "no gas for the next 150 miles." We rolled along on the gravel road and finally it became a dirt road; then you couldn't really say it was a road at all. We came to an area where it was just a ledge that went around the side of the mountain and it was just barely wide enough that my station wagon was able to get around the curves by hugging the mountain. Everyone was on pins and needles. Finally we got out of that area and into an area that was somewhat flat, and once again we were virtually following a deer trail, not really a road. It had never been graded, there were no ditches, and it was just a path. We were able to go a little faster when all of a sudden I came to some very soft sand on the right side with lots of rocks on the ground just beyond the sand. I hit this and it pulled my car sideways, a big rock hit my front right wheel, which not only blew the tire but bent the rim. Another rock took the manifold off the engine, my gas tank dropped from above half a tank to zero, and the engine died. Upon examination, I discovered a rock had gone through our gas tank; I could stick my fist through the bottom of the gas tank.

Here we were in the midst of this vast wilderness; many wild animals, bears, lions, bobcats, not to mention rattlesnakes were in abundance. I looked at my speedometer and we had come 75 miles since we had seen the sign. I had made a note of my mileage and knew there was absolutely not a house, not a ranch that we could see for the 75 miles behind us, so it was decided that my wife would stay with the car as many of our children were quite young, and that my oldest son, Kevin, and second daughter, Glenda, and I would take off walking. They were young themselves.

We walked, and walked, and walked for hours on end. I had a brand new pair of cowboy boots on. Boy, was that a mistake! My feet got blistered, blisters upon blisters, they got raw; I remember stopping and taking off my boots and my feet looked like raw hamburger. I realized I must very quickly get the boots back on or my feet would swell to the point I could never get them on. Swell they did, the blisters broke, my feet bled and we kept on walking. The children had tennis shoes on so it did not bother them. With my history of heart trouble, the longer I walked, the more my chest and left arm were hurting. I remember we had walked so long, we decided that the kids would gather rocks, and we would make a sign in tall letters. It said, "Family in Car" and we made an arrow pointing back to the car for an airplane that may fly by, looking for us. But why in the world would they fly over this horrible wilderness of tall mountains where there was no place to land? Undoubtedly they would search the highways.

We continued to walk, and we saw wild animals run across in front of us on the trail but they did not

73

come after us God's hand of protection was upon us. We thought we saw mirages, but we did not come to water.

Finally after hours of walking we came up over a mountain, and down in the valley I could see a Ranch house, cattle barns and corrals. I began to wonder if that was a mirage also, so I asked the children and they said, "No," they thought it was a house and a barn. We walked and walked and walked, and as we got closer we could see there was a man sitting in a rocking chair on the porch. We began to wave our arms, but he just continued to rock. Finally, hobbling and in terrible pain, not only from my feet but from my chest, we arrived at the porch and I introduced myself to Mr. Don Bartram. He said, "Well, preacher, I have been watching you for a long time. If I had known who it was, I would have come and got you but I figured it was some 'hippies' and I just don't help 'hippies.'"

Well, at any rate he said he would be glad to help us. He became a good friend and later moved near Apache Creek. I told him I had tried to change the tire and put the spare on but I had broken my lug wrench. So he got a heavy duty lug wrench, we loaded in his pickup and I asked him to check the mileage. It was 37 miles through terrible mountain terrain back to where our car was. When we got there he was able to get the wheel off with his heavy lug wrench and we got our spare on. He hooked on and towed us off in another direction 35 miles. I had seen that road but I had thought the best thing was to keep going straight.

When we got there we saw a rock house and the family that lived there. Mr. Bartram knew the man happened to have an old carbide welder. Unless you are an "old-timer," you would probably have no idea what that is. They used to have carbide lamps, and this man had this carbide welder that generated gas as the carbide burned and worked like a cutting torch. They took the gas tank off my car while the lady insisted that we come into the house. She could see that I was in terrible pain; she asked what was wrong and I told her about my feet. We managed to get my boots off and they were a bloody mess. She fixed a bucket of Epson salt and warm water. I sat there with my feet in the salt water while she stoked up the fire in the wood burning stove and fried some potatoes in some bear grease that she had. She had a pot of beans on the back of the stove and some cornbread that had been left over. My, how we enjoyed that meal as it was already well after dark and we had not eaten all day long.

Meanwhile, the men outside with lanterns and this carbide welder had taken the tank off the car, hammered it out the best they could, found a piece of scrap iron, cut a piece out and welded it over the bottom of the gas tank. This all took a great deal of time and it was very late by the time they got finished. By then I couldn't put my boots back on, but had a clean pair of socks that I put on. The rancher had a five gallon can of gas there that he kept for his truck, which he seldom used, and got us on the road.

The family told us many interesting stories while the men were getting the car ready. I asked them if

75

their children went to school and the mother said, "I teach the children myself" (this was a long before the home school movement).

I said, "What about when they get in high school, will you take them off to school?"

A great fright came across her face and she said, "Oh no, I would never ever do that. I was born on this ranch and my mother taught me, but when I got in high school I needed more education so they sent me to live with an aunt in this huge, huge city. It was so awful, so many people. I had a complete nervous breakdown and they had to bring me back to the ranch. I have never been off of it since."

Their ranch was 163 square miles or 163 sections. I thought, "Oh my poor soul, they must have sent her to Chicago or New York or some place." There at the ranch they would see a neighbor maybe once a year when ranchers would get together and help in the branding of their cattle; otherwise she had never been off of the ranch. The rancher would go out every six months and told us it was a good thing that we started walking because he was the only one that ever went down that dirt road. He had gone to the little town a week before and he would not be going again for six months. He would buy gun powder for reloading his shells, salt, flower, and pinto beans and that is pretty much what they lived on. In the summer they lived on beans and potatoes which they grew on the ranch. During the winter they would live on their beans and game that they would shoot. They preferred antelope most of all. They could hang it in the shed and cut the meat off as they needed it, when it was cold. Of course they could not do this during the summer months. There was no electricity, telephones or radio. Even if they had a battery-operated radio they could not pick up any stations. So they had lived a very quiet life to themselves. I said "Where was this city that they sent you to live with your Aunt?"

She said "It was such a big place. The name was Reserve." Well, Reserve is 18 miles from our ranch and has less than 400 people. It is the biggest town in our county. Catron County is so large that you could put two of some of the eastern states in it.

Well, I understood that she would be teaching her daughters. I asked them, "Do you folks own this ranch?"

They said, "Oh no, there is a doctor in Texas that owns the ranch."

I said "Does he ever come and see you?"

They said, "Once he came to see it – he, his wife, and children. They had, like a house on the back of his truck" (of course it was a camper). She said that they were the funniest people. "They would come and eat with us, and after they had eaten then they would go out to that house on their truck, and they had these little sticks that had bristles on them. They would rub them all over their teeth, and the whole family would laugh and laugh." It had been the only time that they had ever seen a toothbrush.

Well finally our car was running. It roared something fierce with the manifold broke off. But it had four wheels and it had enough gas that we were

77

able to make it on to Reserve. They hadn't built the motel there yet, but there was an old hotel. The old hotel was full downstairs but they said they had a room up in the attic. All 11 of us piled up in there. On the bed, on the floor, wherever we could find a place under the eaves, and fell in utter exhaustion.

The next morning we went out to the ranch, and I showed the family around. We had not tried going to the old cabin that night as I hadn't really had a chance of checking it out and seeing what was available. I had just been on the land and prayed for it. The old two-room cabin was made out of 1x12's. In fact there were no 2 x 4's in the walls at all. They built the floor and then they nailed 1 x 12's around the side. At the top they would nail a 2 x 4 and on that they would set the rafters. That made up the two rooms of the house.

Later when we were doing some remodeling we found out that they had gone around the house and nailed a second set of 1 x 12's mismatching the cracks, and used newspaper in between the board as insulation. In 1942 there were lots of newspapers with stories of the war breaking out. They had an old wood-burning stove and a bed in one room. The other room was the kitchen with a wood-burning cook stove.

We found out the house had originally been built in Luna in the mid 1800's about 50 miles away over terrible mountainous roads. Later it was moved to Reserve. I don't know if they took the walls apart and hauled them on a hay wagon or how they did it, but it sat in Reserve where the motel now sits, and where the old hotel sat at that time. Later it was moved to Apache Creek where there was a saw mill. It sat there for some years. Then Grandma Gann bought our ranch. She needed a place to live, and so she bought the old two-room shack down at the Apache Creek Mill which was not in use then, and moved it six miles up to the ranch around 1880 or something like that. So the house is more than 150 years old.

Our son, Craig and his wife Debbie and their three children now live in the house. We built two new bedrooms on the end and then later we put in two bathrooms, another bedroom and sheet rocked the inside. Now we've put in modern cabinets and carpet, and it is a modern home today. When we were building the ranch we took our scraps and nailed them over tar paper on the old wood siding and took the 1 x 12's, 1 x 6's, 1 x 4's, whatever we were using, and nailed them like shingles all the way around the house. It still this way to this day, making the wall three inches thick.

That day, we couldn't stay long because we had to get back for Jake's graduation that night. We hadn't planned on having so much trouble. But we figured out what we would do for the summer camps and hurried back and got him there just in time for his graduation.

The original cabin on the ranch, built in the mid 1800's. Pastor Craig, our son and family, still live in this house, but we have added 3 bedrooms and 2 baths. In early days it was our girl's dorm. Also pictured is our Greyhound bus.

In the beginning the camp boys stayed in tents.

Chapter 6

The Actual Building of the Camp

As I mentioned, the first summer we just brought the kids from our church. We used the old cabin for the girls and tents for the boys. But now we were getting in earnest. The down payment had been made and we needed to build buildings on the camp. My dear friend Elmer Riber from Illinois flew out in January to El Paso. He and I went up to the camp to lay out what we were going to do. We set a couple of stakes and lined up what would be the front of the main buildings of the camp, according to which we have built down through these 30 years.

When we got up there it was extremely cold. We built a fire in the old cabin and stayed there. It got down 30 below zero that night; the coldest I have seen it at the ranch. The next day we went out and started laying things out. We went into Reserve to the City Hall and asked where we could get building permits to build at the ranch. They said, "Well Preacher, there are no building permits. You just go build whatever you want to build and all will be fine." So we went out and began to make plans.

When the weather began to break in the spring I went up to the camp and single handedly built the first building in a day's time. There was a foundation beside the house where the Tuckers apparently had intended to build a garage, but had never built it. I bolted down a plate to the bolts that were already in the concrete, and like they did with the house, I began to nail 1 x 12's (which I got from the saw mill south of Reserve) to the side of the plate and ran a 2 x 4 across the top. I had left room for a double door in the front, a single door in the back, and windows on the side. When I got this all up I began to take the rough lumber and make rafters which I put up. I added a tin roof on it with some tin which I brought from El Paso, and we had a building. This gave us a place to keep our building supplies which we brought up along with our tools.

A little later in the spring, Brother Riber brought out a crew of men from Illinois and a dozer and we put up more buildings. We built a building that was going to be a girl's dormitory on one end and a boy's dormitory on the other end with separate bathrooms in the center. We had the side walls built before Elmer came and put 1 x 12's on them and made the holes for the window. The man at the sawmill who sold me the lumber in those days (I believe it was eight cents a foot) would come out after work and help us nail it up. We had the rafters up but had no roof on it.

I had taken the 2 x 12's that I gotten at the sawmill, dried them out, laid them out on the ground and built giant trusses out of them. I used gallons of wood glue and nailed them. This was to be a long dining hall and church building. When Brother Riber came we put up the side walls, and he used a crane on the end of his bull dozer and we lifted the rafters up in place. Everything was in place when they had to go back to Illinois.

We made it a practice on Friday evenings after school to load a bunch of boys from the church and any men that were able to get off early on our Greyhound bus and we would make the six hour drive to the ranch. In those days we always had to take our Greyhound up through Socorro and across because the roads from Silver City were so bad. It was just too bad to travel with the big bus. At that time there were no fences, it was open range, and as we would be getting in late in the night, I had put a spot light in the top of the bus. I would shine it down the center line so I could see cows asleep on the road, get out and kick them to get them to get off the road so we could go on. We never saw another car for the whole 125 miles.

This particular night we got to the ranch somewhere near midnight, tumbled into the old cabin, found places on the floor to sleep, and built a fire. At sun up the next morning we were up and out, ready to go to work for the day. Usually my daughter or someone would come to cook the food. We went out, and there on the big combination dining hall tabernacle we had built, and on the roofless girl's dorm, there were red tags everywhere. I began to read the red tags and the notes that had been left. They said, "You cannot build anything here. Everything must be torn down." There was a phone number to call, but I couldn't call until I got back to town.

I called, and spoke to a man from Santa Fe who was head of the state board of builders. He said that since our ranch was called "The Apache Deaf and Youth Ranch" that we had to meet hospital standards. I said, "Why does a youth camp have to meet hospital standards?"

He said, "The word 'deaf' is a medical term and so you must meet hospital standards. Well, I don't know if it would have done any good if I would have changed the name of the ranch or not, but I wasn't about to back down, and I don't think he would have either. They came out and literally tore down the huge building with a bulldozer. Though they did not tear down the dorm, they left word for us to tear it down. They had splintered all that lumber. We salvaged what we could out of it and eventually built an arena around which we held bonfires.

Before we got that built and began taking these boys to camp, we would work all day building and then in the evening we would meet around the bonfire and our preacher boys would take turns preaching. But our heart sank. We had been advertising that we were going to have our first deaf camp that year. The year that we took the kids from our own church, we still took the deaf kids to the Bill Rice Ranch in Tennessee. We had sent out letters and asked people if they could help sponsor a deaf child to camp for $35.00. But every week inspectors were there. Every week we were reminded that we could not bring the deaf children onto the ranch property.

This went on, and on, and on for 13 weeks. Every week somebody from Santa Fe, New Mexico, 280 miles away, or from Las Cruces 200 miles away, or from Silver City 125 miles away were there. We were dead in our tracks, so we kept praying, praying and praying. I kept going to the ranch and planning what we would do.

Finally, the postal inspector called me one day and said, "The building inspector from Santa Fe says he found a letter that you had written saying that you were going to have a deaf camp and asking people to sponsor a deaf child for $35 for camp. Is that true?"

I said, "Yes that is true."

He said, "The inspector tells me that you are not going to have a camp. If you do not have a camp you are going to go to prison for mail fraud for asking people to give $35 dollars for a camp that you are not having."

I said, "Sir, we are going to have deaf camp." There was never any doubt in my mind that was going to happen. And yet the building inspectors came. One hinted that if we would give him $2,000 under the table he might give us a plumbing permit. I chased him off the ranch.

Finally, we were down to the week before the deaf camp was going to start. I had contacted the Army and they had agreed to loan me two large army tents and a bunch of cots. Still, the inspectors said that if I brought a deaf child on to that land I would go to prison. One day when I stopped at the Apache Creek

Store, kind of the spit and whittle club, they were talking, and when I walked in, they said, "Hi Reverend, is the state giving you trouble?"

I said, "Yeah I reckon they are."

They said, "Are you going to give in to them?"

I said, "No I don't reckon I will."

They said, "Well, we've been watching you, and we got the idea you weren't just going to bow to them."

I said, "Yeah that's right."

I had been into City Hall one day when the lady ran and pulled the blind down and locked the door. I said, "Why are you closing so early?"

She said, "See that car out there? That white car with the blue plates? Whenever the state shows up here, we are locked up." Well, that was kind of the opinion through out the county of these old ranchers, many of them, perhaps, descendants from the robber's roost that had been there years before.

So the men there said, "Preacher, we've had a meeting and we've decided we're going to help you."

I said, "Well thank you. I can use all the help I can get." You see, back in the old days the outlaws would ride into that canyon and the sheriff's posse would come after them. There would be men stationed on both sides of the hill that would pick off the sheriff's posse until they wouldn't follow them into the canyon anymore, and they were relatively safe.

The ranchers in the store said, "You know we've all got thirty thirty's (guns) in the back windows of our pickups, and we know all those state cars are white with blue license plates." They will never know who shot them." We will just take care of that for yah."

I said, "Well, you've got a point there, but I still have a few things up my sleeve. Why don't you just wait and see what happens?" So they did. I traveled all over the state talking to contractors, trying to talk to state representatives. They all told me that they were afraid of the man at the inspectors department in Santa Fe. We were getting closer to camp, but I was getting nowhere. Here it was, Thursday, and camp would start on Sunday. I still had the threat of going to jail when the deaf kids arrived, and surely they were going to arrive. While I was working around the ranch, somebody came up from the store. They said, "We have good news for you."

"Boy I could sure use some good news."

So, Preston Porter, Buster Alexander and Mr. Milligan from the store said, "We got to thinking about this and we got to remembering, there was an old school teacher we know." At the time, Jerry Apodaca was governor of the state of New Mexico. This was his first term in office; he later came back and ran again for a second term. They said, "This school teacher taught Jerry Apodaca in a one-room country school house when he was a little boy, and we went to see if she had any ideas." I had tried to see the governor, but couldn't get in to see him. So they went and told the teacher what was going on. She became quite indignant. She had a telephone, so she called the governor's mansion and said, "I want to talk to Jerry."

The receptionist said, "Jerry who, ma'am?"

She said "The governor you dummy."

He said, "Ma'am, the governor is very busy and he can not talk to you."

She said, "You go put a piece of paper on his desk, tell him his teacher is on the phone and to pick up that phone now!" Well they did and he did, and he got the tongue lashing of his life. She said "I did not raise you to be like this."

He just sputtered and said, "Ma'am I don't know what you are talking about." And so she told him what was going on. He became very upset. "If you can get word to that young preacher to be here in Santa Fe tomorrow morning at nine o'clock, this will be worked out."

So they came and told me, and I got in my VW and drove to Santa Fe, New Mexico. You would have thought I was some dignitary, as the red carpets were rolled out for me. They couldn't do enough for me. The head building inspector was told to stand back and shut his mouth. They handed me all kinds of building permits, no fees. "Here, have this and this and this, and anything else you want."

This was Friday, camp started on Sunday. We had one outhouse and a bathroom for the girls in the old cabin, and that was it. So I called El Paso where I had some plumbers in my church. I said, "Can you guys be here Saturday and bring up supplies to start putting in a bathhouse?" I had bought an old cement mixer, and we loaded up gravel out of the creek and got ready to pour concrete while they were putting the pipes in for a bath house and a hand-poured cement septic tank. By Saturday night we had the pipes in and the concrete poured, but no walls for the bathhouse. Yes, God had given us the Victory! That was the end of our hassle with the State. I will tell you about the Deaf Camp in the next chapter.

Later in the summer the chief man out of Santa Fe who had been so mean and had threatened to throw me in prison drove in. I said, "Oh no, here we go again." He got out of his car and stood on one foot and then the other. He had been a mean sergeant in the Army, but he was tame as a lamb on that particular day. He cleared his throat a number of times and finally said, "I have got to get this over with. The Governor told me to come down here and apologize to you. I said I would write a letter, but he said the State can't afford the stamp. He told me, 'You will drive down there, and do it in person.'" He got in his car and drove away, and I have not seen him since. Isn't God good? Certainly He is, and He is a rewarder of those who diligently seek Him.

Walls up for new dining hall. No money for cement floor or roof. We put plastic over the roof on one end and used it for our church.

Building is finally finished. We were still using one end for church and the other for a dining hall. This is a group of deaf children about our 3rd or 4th year. Entire building is now our dining hall.

Chapter 7

My First Deaf Camp at the Ranch

As I mentioned, the first year at the ranch was just young people from our own church. We had about 200 teens and about that many young ones. I also mentioned some of the problems of trying to get the camp built, and that our men from El Paso came up and put in plumbing and poured a floor for our bath house. That is as far as it got. Camp opened on Sunday.

We always start deaf camps on Sunday because we need more time. Deaf children who have never been to camp usually have no idea who God is or where they came from or many of the things we take for granted today. We always start out at the very beginning and teach them, so we need extra time for this period. I had my associate preach at the church and I had stayed at the camp that weekend.

Everything was moving rapidly since we had finally gotten permission to build. We had gotten two big army tents from Fort Bliss, Texas and had them up with cots. The little shed that I had built beside the house was where we set up our cooks' stove. Our first year we cooked on the wood burning stove in the old house, but now we had a gas stove set up and a temporary sink and all the cooking was done in this little building. The only restroom facility we had was a small bathroom in the old cabin that the Tuckers had put in, along with a well point that went down twelve feet that gave us water. We did have electricity. For the boys we had a single outhouse. We had no place to assemble, no dining hall, no chapel or anything of that order.

So I had gone on Saturday to the saw mill and got a load of 2 x 12's and 2 x 8's and brought them to the ranch and had spent the remainder of the day pouring cement and getting the slab ready. On Sunday I was busy with the chain saw cutting up the boards to make benches. I put these in front of the old cabin and I thought it was rather ingenious. I made 2 x 12 legs, a 2 x 12 bench, and then the back that came up had a 2 x 8 across it to lean against like a pew or chair bench. I put another 2 x 8 on top, so for the meals you would turn and put your feet backwards and you had a table. It was out in the open and when it rained you could eat soup forever, it seemed. Then you turned around and we had our assembly. I built a little platform at the other end.

I was still working on these benches when a Greyhound bus pulled in. It had come from Tucson, Arizona to Phoenix where it had picked up more deaf, and then on to the ranch. I could tell there was a great deal of discussion going on between a lady on the bus and the bus driver. She was wearing high heeled shoes and silk hose and was not expecting a wilderness camp. She was demanding that the bus driver turn around and take them home, saying that we were not ready for camp.

The day before I had gone to the local telephone man, and told him we needed a phone. The telephone company was brand new, and they had a few wires strung from posts mainly cut from the forest. They did have line on the road past our property and we did have electric poles coming in from the highway to the ranch. He told me it would be impossible to put a phone in because they did not have any poles to run it up to the camp. I told him we have a lot of deaf coming and I thought it was important that I have a phone in case of an emergency. I suggested that he run the phone wires on the existing electric poles. He told me they couldn't do that because the electric company would charge them for using their poles. I said put it up and pay the bill. We need a phone. So he ran the lines. They came up to the camp and were a little below the electric lines but high up on the pole. At the end there were just simply two bare wires. He said, "Now we have another problem, we don't have any phones." The phone company was new and what phones they had had all been used in other areas, not up in the wilderness. He said, "We simply do not have a single phone that we can give you."

I looked at him and said, "What is that hanging on your belt?"

He said "Well, this is my lineman's phone but I have to have this."

I said, "Well since there are no phones out here I don't see that you really need it for this coming week. I would ask that you leave it here for us." He finally agreed and left me the phone. I had gotten a ladder and put it up to the phone line on the electric pole.

Finally the lady had gotten off of the bus, still trying to get the bus driver to take them back. He had explained that he had already driven his allowed hours and he would have to be off for eight hours before he could be on the road again. She came and said, I need a phone to call my husband to come and get me." She was very upset. I was so proud; I handed her the phone and showed her the alligator clamps at the end. I told her if she would climb the ladder and clamp the alligator clamps to the two bare phone wires that she would get a dial signal. I explained to her that she would have to call collect as we did not have a phone number. I can still see her climbing that pole rather rapidly and angrily in her silk hose and her high heels and clipping on and dialing zero. She argued with the operator and said, "These people don't have a phone number, just put me through on a collect call to my husband." Finally I heard her talking to her husband and saying, "You will come and get me right now! I will not spend a night in this place!" Well, it was already afternoon and it was a long 300 miles from Phoenix, and the roads in those days were not as good as they are now. Then she came down the ladder and gave me the phone back.

Soon we had supper and gathered the large group of deaf that had come from El Paso; Tucson; Phoenix; the Los Angeles area; Denver, Colorado; Colorado Springs; Albuquerque; Santa Fe, New Mexico;

Tennessee and etc. We had our first service that evening and the power of God fell upon the service. I remember so well when the service was over the dear lady came to me, crying, saying, "Please I must have the phone again." She climbed the pole, more somber this time, and tried to call her husband. The phone rang and rang, but he was not there. He had realized that she was very upset and had gone and picked up her father and asked him to make the trip with him to Apache Creek, New Mexico. They did not arrive until early the next morning. I can still see the dear lady kneeling beside the car in the dirt with her husband's window open, and begging him not to make her go home. She said, "I can't leave this place, something is happening here." Finally the husband looked at the father, they both shrugged their shoulders, backed out and drove back to Phoenix, Arizona. This dear lady came to the camp for the next seventeen years. She had a deaf daughter that she had brought, and the deaf daughter came until she was grown and married and moved away.

It was a fantastic week. Elmer Simpson was there from Denver, Colorado and brought a group of deaf. Elmer came every year to camp for the rest of his life and always was a big entertainer for the deaf. They called him, "Crazy Elmer." He really was a very intelligent engineer and had invented many things, including the pop-up tents that are so popular today, only he built the big ones that were used by the Air Force as hangers for helicopters, etc. and for the telephone company for men to work in the bad weather up on the lines. I believe Clint Arthur was also there that year from Ohio. He directed our sports as he did for many years. Don and Betty Cabbage had come from the Bill Rice Ranch in Tennessee to help us. Dr. Bill sent some folks to help us with our deaf week for a number of years, and often sent an offering to help as well.

The week went on; we had a fantastic time and great numbers of deaf came to know Jesus Christ as their Savior that week. My wife was doing the cooking in our little make-shift building and everybody enjoyed it as she is a fantastic cook and has been for many years. My oldest daughter, Heather, cooked for many of the work camps. Soon everybody was wishing they could have a shower. While camp was going on we were building the outside walls to the bath house and had the water run to it. By Friday we had the 1 x 12 walls all the way around the bath house. We had not been able to put the slabs over the cracks, but since the wood was just drying they weren't too wide yet. There was neither roof nor ceiling on the building yet. Still, everybody was so thrilled to be able to take a shower on Friday before the evening celebration.

In our deaf camps we use total communication which is voice, sign language, and often visual aids. We have developed many new methods down through the years to reach the deaf and now reach out worldwide with the Gospel to the deaf. The Bible says in Isaiah 18:20 *"And in that day the deaf shall hear the words of the book."* I believe that very much applies to this present age, in which we are living, and that God was with the Apache Creek Deaf and Youth Ranch. No wonder Satan fights us so much. To God be the glory!

Chapter 8

Building Buildings With Men and Boys

Now we got down to building earnestly. Many of the men from the church would come up on the weekends, and many of the boys asked if they could come and help build during the summer months. Each week we would bring a bus load up on our Greyhound, and we had also gotten a truck. Dale Stamford had called and told me there was a Rio dump truck in North Carolina. A friend had the truck in his shop; the owner hadn't paid the $800 repair bill and had never come back to pick up the truck, so we bought the truck. Wayne Owens from our church in El Paso flew out to North Carolina and drove the truck back. It took him a long time to get back; he told me the truck had a top speed of 30 miles per hour. I went out and put a new fuel filter on it and then it ran like a scared rabbit. He kept kicking himself that he hadn't thought about that on the way back.

This big heavy-duty dump truck would pull down into the creek bed, these young men would get up, and

I would say, "Alright fellas, let's go down and load up some gravel." We would take shovels and fill that truck with sand and gravel. Then we would come up and there would be a big breakfast of eggs, maybe pork chops, fried potatoes, and gravy – the works – and boy could the fellas put it away!

I had bought an old cement mixer which had a big hopper on it and made a lot of cement. We would back it up to a form where we had started building cabins up on the hill. I had brought up 100 lb bags of cement in the truck out of Mexico. We would dump the gravel by the mixer and we would mix the concrete and then pour it. All morning long we would pour concrete, and by noon when it was all poured we would stop for a hearty dinner. Then in the afternoon we would do our best to float it out and finish it, though sometimes it wasn't finished smoothly. The old creek sand and gravel pitted over the years and now looks much older than it is.

When we had the floor poured, we would start building a cabin, once again using the old rough lumber we had gotten from the saw mill. The front would be nine feet tall and the back of the cabin would be seven feet tall, giving us a sloping roof back. We would try to build one of these cabins in a week's time and put a tin roof on it. They were 16 x 24; feet, we built a series of eight of these cabins altogether.

My two older sons, Kevin and Brian, and a number of other boys who didn't have jobs worked all summer long doing this, and others would come when they could. Every one of those young men today have top-notch jobs and have done very well for themselves.

They learned to work, they learned to enjoy work, and we had a great time together. Many of them look back on that time with very fond memories.

As we began to get cabins built with roofs on them and got the roof put on our bath house, we were rolling in camps. However, we had to sleep on our sleeping bags on the cement floors in the cabins as we didn't have any beds. Next I started looking for bunk beds that we could get to put into the cabins.

One of the men from the church was driving our big O Diamond Rio, pulling the goose neck trailer that Freddy Elmore had built, on a trip from El Paso when the V-8 blew. The truck got three to six miles per gallon, which wasn't so bad back when gas was 30 some cents per gallon. However, we couldn't find another engine for sometime for the big Diamond truck. Dale Samford told me that the Sword of the Lord in Murfreesboro, Tennessee had a ¾-ton truck that they would donate to us. It was an International crew cab with a lot of miles on it. They had used it to haul the Sword of the Lord and bulk mail to the post office, and send it out all over the country. We got the truck, and my, what a wonderful blessing it was to us! As I said, it was an old truck and it had been well-used. We did have a lot of problems, in fact there are very few roads in New Mexico that I haven't broke down on in that old truck at some time or another, but it hauled many a trip from El Paso (300 miles one way), went back East to get supplies, took kids to college in Indiana, and many other chores.

I heard that there was going to be an army sale at Fort Huachuca, Arizona down near the Mexican border. It was in the summer, so I loaded the boys up and we left one afternoon, and thought we would get down there, camp out for the night and be there for the sale the next morning. Well, the old truck had other ideas and kept breaking down constantly. We finally arrived at Fort Huachuca about 11:30 the next morning. I went in to ask for a bid card so I could bid in the sale and they said, "The sale's nearly over, it is too late."

I said, "Just give me a card, and maybe I can get something." Well I rushed in and they were auctioning off bunk beds, big lots, mattresses and so on. Most of the people had gotten everything they wanted and I was able to buy bunk beds for $1.75 each and mattresses, I believe, for $1.00 each. In the ten minutes I was there I had bought enough stuff that I would spend the rest of the summer hauling it out. Behind this International truck I had the big, old homemade goose neck trailer that Freddy Elmore had built, and we could really put a big load on it. The front part of it was covered so we stacked it with bunk beds as high as we could, and then beyond that we stacked them on up higher so they would just go under the bridges. My, what a load we had! We came out of the Fort and started back home, coming up through Safford and Mule Creek Pass. We came through it in the night time and didn't realize, really what a steep climb it was. Well, we started up this road which has switch backs that make you want to honk at your own tail lights as you go around them and we got part way up the mountain and our truck simply would not make it. I told the boys, "I don't know how long the brakes will hold so everybody jump out, grab a rock and put it under the truck wheels and the trailer wheels," which they did. There simply was no place to turn around and it would have been absolutely impossible to back down. There were drop offs at the edge of the road 100's of feet down. We just had to go on up the mountain.

We raised the hood on the truck and let it cool down as it had very bad problems of vapor locking. We had tried wrapping the gas line with tin foil, we had put clothespins on it, we had used every trick of the trade, but it was always vapor locking. Later, we finally ran the gas line around in front of the radiator and this helped some. But on this particular occasion we would let it cool and then I would say, "Alright, everybody be ready to grab the rocks and move them up." This being a two-seat, four-door truck, we had room for lots of guys and everybody had a rock. I would start the engine, put it into low gear and push it to the floor. Sometimes it would go a foot, sometimes it would go ten feet, and then we would let it cool off again. Some places where it wasn't so steep we would go several feet. Finally, 24 hours later we made it up Mule Creek Pass. My, what a time we had getting up that road!

From there on we drove through the rest of the mountains and finally we got back in the camp in the middle of the night. I shut the truck off and everybody went to a cabin and collapsed on the floor after two long days. It had been extremely hot in Fort Huachuca. The next morning I went out to move the truck around to the cabin so we could start setting up bunk beds, which we all were really looking forward to. The truck would not move; it wouldn't go forward, it wouldn't go backwards. The transmission was totally shot, but it had gotten us home. My, isn't God good!!

Well, we took the transmission, and it was going to be awhile before we could get another transmission to put in the truck. Tom Burks at Wholesale Lumber in El Paso, Texas, rented me his big flat-bed truck, and a young man who had stopped by from California and helped us for a few weeks went with me, and we headed back to Fort Huachuca to get another load of beds. We had this truck stacked high, and I believe there was one other guy with us that helped us load.

When we came out of the Fort it was 120 degrees and we were really exhausted and hot. There was a Dairy Queen there, so I said, "Fellas, let's get a Dairy Queen, maybe it will cool us down some." I don't remember what the other two got, but I got a marshmallow shake, the largest they had, and boy did it taste good on that hot day! I began driving the truck back towards the ranch, and pretty soon my stomach was hurting something fierce. Pretty soon my eye sight was getting bad. I said to the young man from California, "Can you drive a truck?"

He said "I never have."

I said, "Well obviously I'm not going to be able to drive. You get over here, and I will show you how to do it." So I showed him what to do. He took it slow and easy in lower gears and we got back to the camp in the middle of the night. I was really, really sick. I went to one of the cabins, laid down, and felt like I was actually in a fire burning up. I tried to get up, but could not. The next morning when I did not show up for breakfast Mr. Panek, a man that was living at the ranch at the time, came to check on me, and found out that I was in really bad shape. I was blind and I was in terrible, terrible pain. I said, "Call poison control." He called and they began to ask questions; they wanted to know what I had eaten. I said "I haven't had anything to eat, except a marshmallow shake in Fort Huachuca." They replied that marshmallow poisoning was perhaps one of the worst food poisonings that you could ever have.

They took me to a hospital in Reserve which hadn't been used for several years. An old country doctor, who had been a World War I doctor, used it as his office. Old Doc Foster put me in a room, and the poison center in Albuquerque kept telling him what to give me, and he kept feeding me intravenously. The doctor and his wife stayed with me around the clock for two or three days in the hospital. I guess I was the last patient in that old hospital in Reserve. I finally came out of it, but for many weeks after that I was in such tremendous pain, I always walked doubled over.

Eventually we got all the beds that we had bought to the camp, and set up, and now we were ready to handle many other people. As I mentioned we had built what was going to be a large building, 75 feet x 50 feet. It was going to be a girls' dorm on one end and a boys' dorm on the other end. It had a dirt floor and it did not have a roof on it. A trucker at Apache Creek Store loaned us a big tarpaulin, and we stretched it over the roof and started eating in there and using it as a dining hall. In fact, we ended up making it a dining hall instead of dormitories, since we were building the small cabins. Later we were able to raise the money and put a tin roof on the building, and even later pour a cement floor in it, as it had been built like a pole barn.

Today it has a modern kitchen, and will feed 250 people or more easily at one time. We could take some of the storage area and greatly increase that to three or four hundred people easily. Since we did not have a place for services we also met in this building. In time, Farah Manufacturing in El Paso, Texas, had gone through terrible strikes, and quit serving meals. So we bought many heavy tables, wonderful tables with benches, and filled this building full of tables for our dining hall. We had poured a big slab at the camp that we wanted to build a large auditorium on with maybe girl's dorms along the side. We got the concrete poured, but we were not able to come up with the money to build the building. We put up basketball goals at the end and used it to play basketball on for several years.

Chapter 9

The Building Continues and We Finally Get a Chapel

The chapel took a long way about, coming from Michigan where Dr. Russell Anderson used it as a shed for his trucks. At some point he had donated it to the Bill Rice Ranch in Tennessee. They had moved it there, and they put the beams up for the roof, and I believe on one end of the building it was closed in, but had never put sides on it. It was there for many years but they didn't really use it a lot. One day they had a lot of dirt hauled in around their campgrounds, and needed to move it. They asked my friend Dale Samford if he would do the work. He agreed to do the work for the metal building. So he got the work done, and I sent my son in-law out, and they took the metal building down. Dale had an old fire truck, an old International 48 model if I remember right, and a big trailer, and he thought he could put all of this on the trailer.

They loaded it all on the trailer and tied it behind the old fire truck, and my son in-law Charles Aiken started driving it back with our daughter, his wife, following in my station wagon. Well, it was simply was too much for the old fire truck to pull. It boiled and simply wouldn't make the trip. So after a couple of miles they had to turn around and go back. Well, Dale had an old semi truck with a flat bed that wasn't in very good shape, but the truck was in pretty good shape. It was a big white semi with a Cummings diesel in it. So we bought the semi from him, he loaded the steel building on the flat bed, and put the fire truck on top of the steel building. He took the pews apart, and laid them under and around the fire truck, and put a big, old, four-wheel wide front-end International tractor on the back, over the building along with some other farm equipment. It was stacked very high, so he put concrete rebar around the load to hold it securely in place, and welded it. It seemed it was not going to go any place, and it didn't. So Charles got in the truck, and started back to the ranch with Glenda following him. Glenda is our second daughter.

They got into Nashville, and it was pouring rain so hard, somehow they got separated. Charles pulled off at a station and called us. We told him to stay where he was, and found out exactly where that was. Later our daughter tried to find him but she could not. We were happy to tell her we knew where he was when she called us, and gave her instructions on how to get there. They started on out of town, and went a ways and Charles found out that he could turn right, but he was having difficulty making left hand turns, so he called again. I told him to find a shop, that undoubtedly something had worked loose, and the steering mechanism was hitting it when he tried to turn left. So he found a shop, and sure enough the pin that held the springs on was working out and hitting the steering column. So they got that taken care of and they were rolling down the highway once again.

They both needed to use the restroom, so they pulled off at a gas station, and Charles left the truck running and ran in. When he came out, the truck was lying over on its side. It seems that they had just run a new water line through town. With the rains it was soft, and one side of the truck was sitting over it. It sank, and the truck just rolled over on its side. Well, Dale had welded it in place with rebar rods, so everything was still just right where it had been. He called me, and asked me what to do. I told him, we would have to get some wreckers out there. It took about three wreckers and all the money he had left for fuel to get the truck back righted up once again. I had to go to the bank and wire money to him, Western Union, in order for him to get fuel to continue on.

They made it as far as Dallas and then the bearings went out on the back of the truck trailer. We had to fly Charles's brother Ralph Aiken, who also worked for me, to Dallas and have someone pick him up and take him out to where the truck and trailer was. He took tools, bearings and anything that he needed to fix the truck, and helped Charles bring it on in to El Paso. He took it to one of our church members who had a big yard and cranes in El Paso. We cut off the steel bars, and lifted the fire truck and the tractor off, so we could try and get the fire truck fixed. It had a metal tank that was suppose to hold water but it was all rusted out. They took the tank off, and were going to have it fiber glassed, but somebody inadvertently, hauled the tank off with some trash, and we never did get the fire truck working. We finally got the tractor to the ranch after we had gone on to the ranch with the metal building.

Brother Riber came out, as he had so many times, and we poured concrete for our church building, and erected the steel building. You would never know it was a steel building. On the outside we have log siding, and on the inside we have wood siding, and today it is a very beautiful chapel. It was a building that we had needed so desperately. It was big enough that in the back of it we were also able to build a girls' dormitory, and in the lean-to off of that, we built a snack shop and bath rooms for the girls' dormitory. In later years we built onto the front of it and made a big vestibule with modern bath rooms, and down the side of it a nursery and three large classrooms where we could hold special classes. Sometimes we cleared out the classrooms and put mattresses on the floor when we had larger camps and needed more beds. It certainly has been a useful building.

About the same time we poured the cement floor in the dining hall. We built a six-unit motel off of the church building. For quite some time it had six rooms; at first we just had boards leaning over the doors and they had no bathrooms. We did put a small back door in each room, so that when we were able, we would add bathrooms to the back of this building. They started out rough, but today we have modernized rooms for our guest speakers, pastors, families and so on to stay.

We built nice bathrooms across the back ends of them, and a nice porch across the front. Later we were able to build another boy's dormitory, but we were still needing more room for our girls. Ralph Aiken, who I have mentioned, was working in Alamogordo, at Holloman Air Force Base, doing a Government contract job there. He called to say that the building which the Stealth Bomber Pilots met in, before they would take off, was going to be taken down as they had built a multi-million dollar building to replace it. He said "I believe they would give you the building if you will come and get it."

I said "Tell them we want it." He called back and said the building was ours. We took a big flat bed truck, jab saws, and once again lots of guys. Every eight feet we would take off a piece of tin. We just cut the walls of the building into eight-foot wide sections and stacked them on our truck. We made many trips, but we finally got it all to the ranch.

The building had restrooms in one end and offices in the front end. We had to put it back up just the way it came down, as that was how it was constructed. We needed the bathrooms across the back. We had three large bays for the girls in the center part, and what had been the three offices across the front, we made three more motel rooms. Now we have nine motel rooms. We hope in the future to build many more.

Over the years, we would take what money we had, buy what supplies we could buy, and use that to put together all of our buildings at the ranch. When we got more money we bought more, all except for the chapel. A man in Evansville, Indiana wanted to loan me the money to get the chapel all put up at once, which we did, but I wish we had done it like the others. We finally got it paid off, and we are so grateful to have it. This is our camp chapel as well as our year-round church.

In the early days we also built a barn into the side of the mountain where we could keep our saddles, and where our horses could come in. We put hay in the top. We still use this barn today, and recently have built a new modern building that we saddle our horses in for our trail rides. The horses are a very important part of the ranch.

Our schedule is we have devotions in the morning, go to breakfast, clean the cabins, have a service, have free time at the snack shop, another service, and then we eat dinner. By the way, since it is a ranch, we eat breakfast, dinner, and supper — always a little confusing to the city kids. In the afternoon we have horseback riding, sports, mountain hiking, etc.

Usually around the 4th of July the monsoon season starts. About two o'clock every afternoon when everything was getting under way it would rain, and there was no place where they could have sports or places for the young people to go.

Our next to youngest son, Brent, who lived in Orlando, Florida, was a hotel engineer. He fell 11 stories in an accident which took his life in 1994. He was a very outstanding young man. He had just turned 24, and had bought his first house when he was 21. We miss him so much. We will see him again one day in Heaven. I preached his funeral. In memory of him we raised money, and built the Brent David Lang memorial gymnasium which is 75 feet x 70 feet, and is such a blessing during these rainy spells, as well as any other time. We also bought out a skating rink, which had been the largest skating rink in the United States, in Albuquerque. That is where we got many of the skates so we could have skating in the gym in the evenings. We have seats along the side, so we can have special meetings in there, and it serves many, many purposes.

Dr. Dean Lang preaching.

Our present tabernacle on the inside. Pictured is Pastor Burt Blackburn and young lady singing.

Chapter 10

Long Drives Between El Paso, Texas and Apache Creek, New Mexico

As I have mentioned, I was the pastor of a church in El Paso, Texas, which is 300 miles from Apache Creek, New Mexico. During the camp seasons we would leave Sunday night after church and get to the ranch in the wee hours of the morning. Usually late on Friday night our family would leave the camp and start back for El Paso. Often it would be 11:00, 12:00, at night when we would start back, and it would nearly be morning when we got back home. If I was driving the Greyhound bus, it would take a couple of hours to deliver everybody back to their home.

We would spend the day going to wholesale houses, buying groceries, and put as much as two tons of groceries under the bus and on a pick up. Then we would load it up again on Sunday. My wife was busy getting the laundry done and everything ready to go back.

When camps weren't going on I still made constant trips back and forth to the ranch. Virtually I did not go to bed two nights a week, especially through the summer months. Even when camps were not in session, I usually traveled at night so I wouldn't miss any working time at the ranch or at the church. Some of these trips were rather humorous, though not always at the time.

I remember when someone had given us a piano for the camp, and I had it in the back of the International truck which I have mentioned. I also had a steel rack on the back, and on the other side I had a donkey, which I had bought at an auction from the border patrol. His name was Fred; old Fred had been used to smuggle drugs from Mexico into the United States. When he was caught the owner had to forfeit him. He was sold at auction, and I had bought him I loaded the piano and the donkey up, and started out for the ranch one evening after I had done church work all day.

As I was going through the mountains north of Glenwood, suddenly my lights starting getting dimmer, and dimmer, and dimmer. It was a very winding, treacherous road with big drop offs on the side. Finally the truck died and that was it. There I sat in the middle of the highway, on a night when there were absolutely no stars or moon. It was so dark you couldn't see your hand in front of your face. I set the brake and got out, fearful that someone might come down the road, though usually I would drive the 125 miles from Silver City on and never meet or see a vehicle.

I had a flashlight, and after several hours I could hear a truck groaning up through the mountains. I turned the flashlight on, and begin to wave it so he would not plow into the back of the truck. The truck stopped. It was a truck from Ross Caterpillar in El Paso that was going to some mines over in Arizona to work on a big diesel engine. I asked if he could give me a jump, which he did, and we got the truck started. However, when I turned the headlights on, the engine died again. So I asked him if I could charge it a little longer, and I left the lights off. He said, "I don't know what good this is going to do you, because you cannot drive in the dark."

I said, "I've got a plan. There is no one on this road, so if you will drive behind me, and straddle the center line I will be able to see."

He said "That would be fine, except I've got to hurry as I've got to be in Arizona at the mine when the sun comes up, to get that big engine running."

I said, "You drive as fast as you want and I will stay ahead of you." Boy did we zip up through the mountains that night! The old piano and the donkey were rocking back and forth, and it sounded at times like old Fred was playing the piano. This was fine until we got up to the Y where you turn off of 180 onto route 12 to go in through Reserve, and on to Apache Creek. When I turned away from him, having charged the battery a little longer the last time, I would flick the light on just enough to see where the road was. I crept along slowly. When I could feel the truck starting to run off the road, I would flip the light on just enough to get back on. I finally made it to Reserve where there were street lights.

I got on out of Reserve and was trying to make my way to the Ranch. I had gone more than 11 miles out of Reserve when I flicked the lights one last time, and the engine died. It so happened I was in a curve, and I had run off the side of the road. Though I was going very slow, the truck leaned over in the ditch. Well, with the piano leaning against the donkey, he was having a fit. My flashlight batteries had long since run out, and so I was trying to feel the road as I could not see it at all, and make my way on to Apache Creek. I knew the Milligans lived in the back of the store, and I was hoping they would call the ranch, and someone would bring me a battery.

When I got there, I knocked on the door and no one answered. I called out for Mr. Milligan, and his wife opened the door. She was glad I called out because she was afraid to open the door as her husband was out of town, but she recognized my voice. She called the ranch and the family that was living there took a battery out of the tractor and brought it down to the truck. We put it in, and made the journey on, and was Fred ever glad to get out of the truck with that piano!

Fred was a main stay at the Ranch. He could be an ornery old donkey, but he was a loving donkey too. He loved the snack shop. We always kept a good supply of tootsie rolls in the snack shop, and whenever the snack shop was open, here would come Fred running lickety split, standing there hoping one of the campers would buy him a tootsie roll, which they did because they loved to see him chew and chew on it. They got enjoyment, and he loved the tootsie roll. Sometimes in the spring when the campers hadn't been there all winter, Fred was a little cantankerous. But a short two by four, with a little discussion between the ears, and he promised to be a good boy the rest of the summer.

The group from New York sold Fred. I had tried, and tried to track him down. The first woman that bought him said that he ate all her clothes off the line, and she sold him to someone else. I went to see them, and they said that he had eaten all of the flowers, and they sold him to somebody else. I went to see them, and they said some people from Mexico came along, and they sold him, and so he is probably back where he came from. I never found my friend Fred the donkey again.

On another occasion we took the big old Rio dump truck and went to buy hay down near Glenwood. The bed wasn't too long, but it had a big headache rack that went out over the cab, and we would stack hay on that, as well as in the bed. The first time we did it, we got it stacked a little bit too high. We had to go under an old iron bridge, but when we got to it, it would not go under the bridge. The boys with me climbed up on top, threw down the top row of hay, and we drove across the bridge. Boy was it hard stacking it back up at that 12 or 13 foot level, but we made it, and our horses had hay.

We were constantly building, and we would take the old semi that we bought off of Brother Samford to Juarez, Mexico, where we would load it with 100 pound bags of cement. We got too many bags on it one trip. We came back to the border crossing, went through immigration, and went on, but the truck sat still. The weight had sheared all the lug bolts off. We managed to get someone to pull us off to the side. We had to rent a U-Haul truck and put as many of the front bags in it as we could. We bought new lug bolts, put them in the truck, and finally got the load to the ranch. Those trips were something else.

As I would drive the bus back and forth, I had a bull horn: a PA system that had a curly wire and a microphone. Often I would preach as I drove down the highway. We had some great times of singing and preaching. It always made the trips go faster.

One particular occasion when I had a large load to go to the ranch and our truck had broken down, Freddy Elmore rented me a new truck to take the load up and back. We were going along north of Silver City. I had Brother Demlow, our school Principal, with me when all of a sudden three big mule deer jumped out across. One of them hit the head light and broke its neck. We stopped and got out. The load was stacked high, but I hated to see the deer go to waste. I didn't have a pocket knife or anything to cut it up, and Brother Demlow, though he was a very big man was afraid to touch the dead animal. I couldn't get it up on the load by myself, so we had to go off and leave it. I thought, "Well thank goodness it didn't do anything but break out a head light. That won't be too hard to fix." The next morning when the sun came up, we saw that the back of the deer had swung into the back of the bed, and it had caved it in all the way back. Sorry about that Freddy!

Freddy and Bonnie Elmore played many important roles in the early days of the ranch. They came and helped us with our cowboy cook outs, our rodeos and many other things. We drove that trip between El Paso and the ranch so many times I could literally drive it in my sleep.

Finally in 1995 we decided that with my health being poor we simply couldn't continue to make these trips, and so when camp was over in the fall I started clearing land to build our house. We had lived in room six for many, many years. We had gotten housing for all the rest of the staff except for us. When my parents passed away they left money so that we could build a house at the ranch.

Our third youngest son is handicapped. When he was three years old he drank paint thinner that some painters had left out, and it has affected his life. He really loves the Lord and is a big help at the camp. We wanted to make sure that he had a place to live. So, by doing the work ourselves, we were able not only to build our house, which also contains the ranch offices, but also a small house for him. I took the backhoe, and began to clear out a spot for both of our houses, and to dig a five-foot deep crawl space under the houses where you could walk stooped over. By Thanksgiving we had the logs laid for both of our houses.

I was having a great deal of trouble of breathing in El Paso, because the pollution from El Paso and Juarez, Mexico, had gotten so bad. I would preach on Sundays, then go back to the ranch on Sunday nights and come back home on Friday nights. By the time camp was over the next year, one year from the date I started, I had finished both houses and we moved to the ranch.

We took our church that was left there and merged it with another church, and actually moved the church with us to the camp. It has been a real blessing there, and we have seen our church grow, and we certainly don't miss those long trips every weekend back and forth to El Paso!

We still do a great deal of driving as our nearest drug store is 85 miles away in Springerville, Arizona. They also have a supermarket there. If we wanted to go to Wal Mart we could go south 125 miles to Silver City or north 125 miles to Grants, New Mexico. There is word that they are going to build one in Socorro as well, which is 125 miles to the east. We also make lots of trips to Silver City for doctor's appointments, hospital visits, etc. We do have a wonderful clinic in Reserve, and Dr. Nebblett is one of the best doctors I've gone to. You just have to make sure you get sick between 8:00 a.m. and 5:00 p.m. Monday through Friday. They also have one of the most outstanding Emergency Medical Services there for the state of New Mexico. We are very fortunate in that we also have a small grocery store in Reserve, 18 miles away, and at Apache Creek they have a very small store only 6 ¼ miles away. If we need anything that is major we have to go to Albuquerque, 200 miles away, or El Paso, 300 miles away. We still get lots of driving done.

Chapter 11

The Airplane and the Semi Load of Horses Face to Face

Sometimes truth becomes more bizarre than fiction, as it often has with us. We had a large group of deaf from El Paso, and another large group from Tucson, Arizona, that wanted to come for deaf camp. My son-in-law, Charles Aiken, took our Greyhound bus loaded with deaf from El Paso, then went to Tucson, finished filling the bus up, and brought them on to camp along with many other groups. It was a wonderful week of camp: many souls saved, and many blessings. God worked in a wonderful way. When camp was over, we loaded the Greyhound bus, and Charles took off with all the deaf going back to Tucson first, down through Mule Creek Pass. He also had three older hearing boys with him to help.

We rushed home in the pick up so that we would be able to get supplies and get ready for the next week, as well as services on Sunday. I had just walked in the door when the phone was ringing, and it was a New Mexico State Police. They said, "There has been an accident with your bus."

I said, "What happened? Did it run off a cliff?"

"We don't know."

I asked, "Is anybody hurt?"

"We don't know."

"Where is it?"

They said, "The people that called us said it was on Mule Creek Pass, off of 180, and that is all they knew." As far as I know they never did go check it out. I immediately called my friend Pastor Atchley, in Silver City, and asked if he would take his church bus and go up, find out what had happened, and bring the folks back to his church. After calling several folks in Tucson and Silver City, and making arrangements for them to send cars over to pick up their groups and their belongings we headed back to Silver City with one of our school buses following. When we got there, they were all back at the church, and they told us the story.

Charles and my sons Kevin and Brian, along with Angel, had stayed with the bus as there had been some problems. The bus did not wreck, it simply just quit running, so they coasted off to the side and stopped. There was a pick-up load of drunken cowboys that kept driving back and forth hooping and hollering and shooting guns in the air, with buckets over their heads so that they wouldn't be recognized. Charles had gotten everybody down on the floor of the bus, and the last time they went by they actually shot into the bus, but no one was hurt. They left and we had no idea who they were. They had sent messages with Pastor Atchley to what had happened to the bus.

Early the next morning, after we got the deaf back to El Paso and delivered home I was at the GMC Dealer to ask what would cause a Jimmy Diesel to quit like that. They thought it was a little pin that went in the injector pump that costs about 95 cents, so we bought the part. Charles's brother, Ralph Aiken, who worked for me, also flew for a cattle company. They would let us use the plane when he wasn't flying for them, if we bought the fuel, for a tax write off. We went to the airport, got in the airplane and flew up to where the bus was supposed to be. Sure enough it was there, and when they heard us buzz over head, they all got out and started waving at us.

We went up and down Highway 180 and saw that there was nobody on it. We went up and down Mule Creek Pass, and saw that there was nobody on it, and so we landed on the highway. The road goes down, and then swoops back up at the top of another hill. We were able to land, stop, and turn around before we got to the crest of the hill. We taxied back to the bus, and rolled the plane off to the side of the road in the ditch. We put the part in the pump, and sure enough it fired right up, and was ready to head back to El Paso. I told Charles to drive up to Highway 180, and block the highway off there, so no one could come in, and sent Angel, as he was the oldest of the boys, to go down the highway over the hill. I said "If anyone should come, make sure that you stop them, and tell them that there is a plane taking off, as we will not be able to see them over the hill." So, he went way down the highway, and we gave him plenty of time. We got the plane back up near the bus, and gunned it, as we

123

knew we had to be in the air when we came to the top of the next hill. We were really pouring the coals to it down the middle of the highway, and just as we got to the crest of the hill, much to our horror, there was a semi truck with a load of horses. The driver's eyes were wide, his mouth was open, and he was screaming. He jerked his truck to the right, we banked to our right, and instead of the propeller going right through his windshield, we cleared the cab as we went over. We retracted our wheels and went back to El Paso.

When the bus finally got back I said, "Angel why didn't you stop that truck?"

He said, "Preacher I tried and tried to stop that truck! I saw him coming way off, and I kept waving for him to stop, but he didn't even slow down. I took off my white shirt, and was waving it frantically, and he would never slow down! He rolled down his window and said a bad word to me. He said 'I don't pick up Mexicans.' I saw him go to the crest of the hill just as you got there. I was sure the propellers were going to go through his windshield,.we just missed it. He locked the brakes on the truck, came back, and hugged me, crying, saying, 'Son I'm so sorry, I'm so sorry. I will never pass up anyone like that again. I will pick up every Mexican I see hitchhiking. I know you were trying to save my life.'" He learned a bitter lesson that day, and we were all very grateful that it turned out as it did.

Chapter 12

Pastor Lang Vs. Mr. Lion

Along with our building in the early days, I must relay this story to you. After our young men had filled the Rio dump truck with gravel, had breakfast, poured concrete, had dinner, finished it off and had supper, we would gather around the bonfire under the big elm tree, and the young men would take turns practicing preaching.

At this point, the old barn and the old cabin were the only two buildings, outside of the outhouse, on the ranch. The barn had a corral around it. In those days we didn't have any money for horses; their upkeep would have demanded a caretaker, but we had some donkeys, as they pretty much take care of themselves. I mentioned bringing Fred to the ranch. We brought another donkey up with the kids, in the Greyhound bus, so we had two grey and black mares. Both of them had babies. By the way, you may have noticed donkeys have a black strip down the center of their back, regardless of what color they are, and another black strip that comes down over their shoulder and fades away. They say that this is because Jesus rode a donkey down the Mount of Olives into Jerusalem on Palm Sunday as he prepared to go to the cross of Calvary.

It was a clear night, with a bright moon, and the young men were enjoying preaching. All of a sudden, there was the most ungodly cat cry that you could imagine, and it was close by. I knew exactly what was going on, that a lion was fixing to eat the donkey colts in the corral. I didn't have any kind of a gun or anything at the ranch, but grabbed up a rough 2 x 4, and being much younger then, I took off running for the corral and jumped over the fence. There he was. This huge mountain lion ready to attack and have one of our colts for his evening supper. I didn't think that was a very good idea, and without giving any thought to the danger, I was determined that I was going to save our colt. I ran towards him with all my might with the 2 x 4, ready to swing and hit him between the eyes. At the last moment, he jumped over the fence and into the field, and I jumped right over after him. He turned and snarled at me and swatted, and in the moonlight I could see his claws extending out of his paw as he swiped. It was too late to be afraid. It never entered my mind. I was determined I was going to get that lion before he got our colts, so I continued to head on towards him, ready to swing. He jumped just as I swung, ran a short distance, turned back, growled a roaring growl, and swatted at me once again. I didn't mind, I was going to make sure he left our colts alone.

We went like that all the way across the field, down to Lee Russell Canyon, where we now have our house. Every time I would just about make contact with the

2 x 4 at the snarling, swatting lion, he would jump and run back a ways. Finally we got to Lee Russell Canyon, and he went into the canyon that was darkened by the shadow of the moon. I felt like he was in his territory, and I wasn't about to follow him up the canyon. I made my way back to the corral, and sure enough, the mothers and both of the young colts were in good shape.

We finally did get some horses. Mrs. Elmore's brother was the sheriff in Farmington, New Mexico, and would allow me to stay with him when I would make trips up to see a chiropractor there. I had asked him if he knew where I could buy some good Indian horses. He said he did, and we made the arrangements. The next time I came up, the man with the horse was there. His name was Mr. Key, and he had four fine-looking two-year-old horses.

There was a palomino that we called Pal. He was a two year old, and wasn't very big, but he eventually grew into quite a large palomino horse, and was as gentle as a teddy bear. There was another one that was a buckskin mare. What a beautiful horse she was! She was my favorite; the one I always road. Then there was a black mare, another fine horse, and a paint gelding. What a spirited animal he was! The horses that you get from the Indians are usually not much of a problem to break, because from the time they are colts, they put their children upon their backs. They seem to grow up with some of the children riding on them. So it was pretty much a matter of putting a saddle on them, waiting until they got a little bigger, and then riding them.

That is, except for the paint. He had a mind of his own and would rear up and try to paw you with his front feet. I decided we had to do something about that. So I tied him to a post where he could not rear up and gave him some feed and a bucket of water. I would keep coming out to see him and pet him until finally he would calm down. He became an excellent riding horse. He had his quirks, but as long as you had tension upon the bridle and he could feel that you were in charge on the saddle, he was at your command. If you ever relaxed for just a second in the saddle, or dropped the reins, you never knew when he would jump out from under you. He didn't buck you off. Rather, he squatted down quickly and reared up on his front feet, and you found yourself lying on the ground behind him. This happened to almost everybody who tried to ride him that forgot, and relaxed. In fact, the last horse I ever rode was the paint; my beautiful buckskin mare had died.

When I was in the hospital in El Paso, and was very ill, one of the men of the church had gone up to the ranch, and wanted to feed the buckskin some grain. He got a bucket, but did not know that it had fly bait mixed in it. He put in some oats, she ate them, it poisoned her, and she died. They were all afraid to tell me that my horse had died, as I was in the hospital having such terrible heart problems. I really miss that horse, and have always wanted to get another buckskin since that day, but the last horse I ever rode was the paint.

I got a 16 millimeter movie camera and began filming around the ranch. I would ride from event to event on the horse, and take movies, and it was making a beautiful film. This film was later confiscated by the group from New York, and I don't have any copies of it, nor the camera. One day, after taking these movies, I was riding by the snack shop, and somebody hollered out, "Pastor, how would you like to have a diet coke?"

I said "That sounds good." It was a hot day, so I stopped the horse, reached out, and got the soda while keeping tension on his reins. It tasted so good! I was so hot and so thirsty! Without thinking, I relaxed. Well, I saw the horse was gone, and I was lying on my back. I had really injured my back. After several trips to the chiropractor to get it straightened out, I finally got back on my feet again, but that was the last time I rode a horse.

Especially in the early days, we did have a lot of trouble with the lions and our horses. We had a number of yearlings that were killed by mountain lions. We also had an older team of mules that the Sheriff's Posse in El Paso had given us, and the lions got them. We learned to respect the lions. We would take trail rides up through Lee Russell Canyon, and if the horses seemed jittery, we would always turn around and come back, as they could smell the lions before we could. It is not a good thing to be on the back of a horse when the lion comes down off of the cliff to clamp his jaws around the horse's neck. It might be your neck instead of the horse's.

Lions do play an important role at our camp. We had an old lion called "Three Toes" who came around quite often at night. He was called Three Toes because he had been caught in a rancher's trap, and only had three toes left on one paw, which made him easy to track. He was a big lion, and one winter when no one was at the camp he slept in the old cabin, and we could see where he had held up during the winter. Often after the pool was built the girls would look out their window and see him coming to the pool at night to get a drink. I remember one night I was asleep in room number six, when all of the sudden there was a terrible crash against the head of my bed. On the other side of it was a little workshop where we had a saw. This lion had chased a deer into the shop, and caught it on the other side of the wall where my head was. I looked out the window, and in a little bit here came the lion dragging the deer up into Goat Mountain Canyon.

The lions only come into the camp during the night, after everything settles down. They are probably the best friends that we've got. When you have a youth camp with a lot of teenage boys and girls, sometimes they are prone to want to slip out at night and meet one another. In the pulpit I have a deer leg. This deer was killed out in front of the church some years earlier by a lion. All I have to do is to hold up the deer leg, which is just bones and a hoof, and tell them that the lion killed the deer out in front of the church at night. I tell them it is not a good idea to want to sneak out of their cabins at night to meet someone, as we would hate to send a boney leg home to their parents. It works every time, and we don't have problems with people wanting to sneak out.

Thank God for the mountain lions! We also have bears around the camp. This summer we had a bear come into the camp several mornings just before sun up. My wife took a picture of him one morning as he climbed the tree, while I held the light on him. We also have lots of elk, deer, and in the plains, antelope. We have a lot of wild pigs and wild turkeys that sometimes come down to the camp when there is no one there. It sure is beautiful to live in the mountains and to see all of this wildlife.

Chapter 13

Serious Health Problems and More

Since my first heart attack at the age of 15, my life has been a series of health problems. It was a constant struggle through college and through each of my pastorships: when I would feel good things would grow, and when I would get very sick things would slow down, but I never let anything stop me. I continued on serving the Lord.

One day, my wife and I had taken a group of elderly ladies in our church to a cafeteria for lunch where they had a wonderful time of fellowship. We were on the I-10 freeway heading back to take them all home in bumper to bumper traffic, when I suddenly realized I was blind. I reached over and shut the ignition off on the van; horns were blaring everywhere. My wife said, "What are you doing? What are you doing?"

I said, "I am blind and I am very sick." She helped me out of the driver's seat and over to the passenger seat and drove home. The ladies helped to get me out of the van and onto my bed. There I lay for a week. It was the beginning of the many strokes that I had over the next three years. Actually, it had started before this. While working at the church and working at the camp and during the many trips back and forth, I had increasingly gotten severe headaches. They would hurt so bad I could hardly stand them; they sometimes made me sick to my stomach. I would take hot showers, I would take cold showers, I would take pain killers, but nothing would seem to relieve the headaches.

I remember in the fall that my wife and I had made a trip back East to see our youngest daughter. She had just graduated from Hyles Anderson College while her husband still had a year to finish up. She was working for Dr. Streeter. I had not been feeling well, and when she got to work she told Dr. Streeter about it. He told her to call me, and to tell me to get over to the office, that he wanted to see me. Reluctantly, I drove over, and my daughter came in and took my blood pressure. She became very quiet and went to get the head nurse. The head nurse came, and took my blood pressure, and also left very quiet. Pretty soon the doctor came in, and he again took my blood pressure. He said, "Do you realize your blood pressure is 250 over 150?"

I said, "No I had no idea. I remember as a boy sometimes, I would get sick and the doctor would say that my blood pressure was very low, so I never dreamed that there was problem with high blood pressure." He ran some more tests, and we went back home.

He called us in El Paso and said he felt there were some serious problems. He asked if I would go to the hospital and have a 24 hour kidney test on my kidneys, and come back to see him. I flew back to Chicago, took a bus, and became very ill on the bus. Somehow I finally ended up at the doctor's office. He checked me and immediately put me in the hospital. I was in near total kidney failure. I remember lying in a bed far away from home. I was so cold! They had blankets piled on me, heating pads, and the furnace turned high, but I shook so violently that my bed walked across the room and blocked the door, and the nurses couldn't get in. Finally they got my bed pushed away.

The next day they took me into the operating room, inserted a camera and dye into an artery in my leg, and inserted dye into my heart and both kidneys. When they took the camera out, I vaguely remember that the blood was spurting so hard that the doctors and nurses were covered, and it was splattering the ceiling. The pressure was so high they just couldn't get it to seal up. Incidentally, it was during this time that someone broke into my locker and stole my wallet with what little money and credit cards I had. I stayed with my daughter and underwent a series of treatments at Dr. Streeter's office. I then went back home, but my health problems weren't over. They kept trying different blood pressure medicines, but none of them would work. The strokes started on I-10 that day and got much worse.

I told you in the first chapter about a time when I was out working on the church by myself. Another rather amusing instant, if there is such a thing, with the many strokes. We had moved out of our beautiful church and into a shopping center in a better area. I was working in my office at church, and I was feeling bad. I had gone over and laid on the couch, and apparently had been out for several hours. I remember I could hear a phone ringing in the distance. I finally realized it was my office phone and managed to answer it. I did not realize it was late in the night. It was my wife saying, "Where are you? What's wrong, why haven't you come home?" It was a Saturday night, and I had been preparing my sermon.

I said, "Oh, I will be there in a little while." I remember locking the church door and staggering across the parking lot. At this time we were meeting in a shopping center because the problems had grown so severe where we were. I remember I dropped my truck keys, and when I bent over to pick them up I fell to the ground. Across the way there was a bar. There was a man coming out who saw me fall, and rushed over to help me up. He said, "Are you alright?"

I said, "No sir, I don't feel well."

He said, "Yeah it does the same thing to me when I drink too much." I got in my truck and went on home.

These problems got worse, and worse. During 1987, 1988, and 1989 I was down more than I was up. I made a trip to Dr. Evers' clinic in Alabama, at the insistence of a friend. I had the money to pay for one week, but when Dr. Evers saw the condition I was in, and I told him I had no more money and it was time for me to go home, he insisted that I stay on, and paid for the next month out of his own pocket.

The clinic helped me a great deal, especially the hyperbaric oxygen chambers. They would put me in these chambers and pressurize me with pure oxygen for an hour, sometimes two hours at a time. It was a glass cylinder; my shoulders rubbed both sides, and the end closed like a pressure cooker. I remember lying there counting dots on the ceiling. But in time I got used to it; in fact I really enjoyed it because it made me feel so much better. I took chelaton treatments every day, and went through every physical thing you could imagine. They tried different blood pressure medicines, but I could not get my blood pressure down.

I came home feeling better. I was able to work, and the church started picking up once again. Then I became very ill. I broke out with boils from my waist, to the top of my head, and was having the headaches and heart problems. I went back to Dr. Evers' clinic, as he invited me to, and there I stayed six weeks, over Christmas even. They took samples of the boils and sent them off, trying to find something that would cure them. Often I would sleep on my knees and elbows, the pain was so severe. I was reminded of Job, and that God saw him through it, and I kept on going. My health improved some, but the boils lasted for a year. Just as suddenly as they came, they suddenly left, but what a year it was! It got to where I was able to preach less and less, and my friends would fill in for me.

Don Cabbage moved to El Paso, and cancelled many of his meetings to preach for me when I was so sick. After two years of this, I had gotten to where I walked with a walker and was nearly an invalid.

Evangelist Charlie Hand had come for a meeting, and was very concerned for my health. He had been a friend of many years. Later he called me, and told me that he was going to work with a children's ministry for a T.V. preacher, back in New York State- there is no point in mentioning the name. He made numerous calls and found out I was weaker and weaker. I had gotten so weak I was pretty much an invalid, and it was difficult for me to walk even from the living room to the bedroom. He called one day and said, "This man has lots of money. He has lots of people working here, good people, and does not have enough jobs to keep them all busy." I told him about you, and he said he wants to help."

Well the T.V. evangelist flew out; he had his own private jet. He said he was so concerned and he wanted to help. He said he would send the staff to help run the camp in the coming summer. Since I hadn't been able to preach, it was difficult for those trying to keep it going, and it was really dwindling down. He said, "I will even send an associate to help you here at the church, so you don't have to worry when you are not able to preach." I had gotten so weak, in fact, that in that coming year I was able to preach once at the church, and none at the camp. It looked like my life was pretty much over. The associate he sent was a good singer, and people enjoyed his singing.

I had to go to the hospital in Juarez, Mexico, for some surgery, because I couldn't afford it in the U.S. I came back, and was able to get out to the church. I found that all the locks had been changed, and the Temple Baptist Church sign had been taken down, and the name of the organization, Freedom Bible Church, was across the front. Things were not right, but I was too weak to do anything about it. I remained mostly at home unable to do anything. Finally I went to a doctor in Juarez, Mexico, that I had gone to on many occasions for allergy shots, as the allergy season had gotten bad. He gave me the allergy shots, and checked me over. He asked me to step back and stand in front of an old fluoroscope machine he had. He said, "You've got to go see a heart specialist here." I didn't much see the point in it as I was going to the best heart, and lung specialist in El Paso, but he insisted.

So I went to the heart specialist, and he checked me over, and wanted to know what I was taking for my blood pressure. Well, I had been through all of the medications, many of them with bad side effects. He said, "We've got a new medicine here that is not available in the United States. I would like to try you on it." He put me on it, and my how it worked! Within one week my blood pressure had dropped 100 points. I hadn't seen it below 250 over 150 since my daughter had first checked it in her doctor's clinic. Often it would get up around 300 over 185 plus the constant stokes, and now it dropped down to 150 over 90. I could hardly believe it. I felt like I was alive again. I still take this same medication, and can now get it here in the States.

In the early spring of 1990, I asked a friend to drive me to the ranch, as I still did not feel safe driving, and had hardly been able to drive for the last two or three years. He drove me to the ranch, and when we got there, there were two ranchers there looking around.

I got out, and said hello to them. One of them said, "Where are all of these things you have for sale?"

I looked at him, puzzled, and said, "I don't have anything for sale." They went back to the truck, and got a sale bill that listed virtually everything we had. The sad thing is that most of it had already been sold. I was flabbergasted!

They looked at each other, and looked at me and said, "Pastor Lang, you didn't know what they were doing to you?"

"No, I didn't know."

I went to a phone and tried to call the T.V. evangelist, in upstate New York, but he would not take my call. All of our horses were gone, all of our hay had been hauled off, and all of our saddles were gone. Our trucks, our tractors, our buses were all gone. I went to the dining hall, and nearly all of our utensils, and many of our tables had been sold. I went to our motels. They were stripped to the bare floors. All of the furniture, even the carpets, had been sold off of the floor. I went to the dorms and many of our bunk beds had been sold. I went to our snack shop, and everything was gone, and so it was, all over the ranch. We were down to empty buildings and bare land. My, how my heart sank!

I called a lawyer, and he said, "It is going to be a real problem. You are going to have to have a lawyer in New Mexico, but you are also going to have to have a lawyer in New York. It is going to cost you far more than you will ever get back from them, I'm afraid." I went to El Paso. They knew now that I knew. The associate had announced that he was moving the church to a new building, and he took more than 400 of our members with him, along with most of the PA equipment and a lot of the furniture, especially folding chairs. The buses we had at church had all been sold, and were gone. When they knew that I had found out, they had acted very quickly.

There were about 35 people that stayed with me in the church. Now that my blood pressure was down, I was able to preach once again, but there were only about 35 people in this large auditorium, and our building payment was $3,500 per month. We struggled on for a few months, and realized that we were not going to be able to do it alone. We rented a small place in a shopping center, and rented our church out to Calvary Chapel as they were looking for a larger place. They paid the $3,500 a month rent, which made our building payments each month.

I set out to try to have camp, as spring was approaching. The electricity had been shut off because the electric bills had not been paid; the phone also. We tried to have camp, but the TV evangelist was determined that he was going to keep me from doing it. He had tried to sell the land, though he had no title to the property. He had tried to put the title of the church in his name. An anonymous caller told me, and we had to go to Austin, Texas, and get it all straightened out. The bank hired a lawyer to help us get everything squared away at their own expense. Yes, my years of being friends and being honest with the bank had paid off.

The first group came to camp, but because we had

no horses for their kids to ride, had virtually nothing at the camp, no motel beds to sleep in, a pastor that had been coming for years and years asked if he could have his money back for his kids, and I gave it back to him. Ed Kollmeyer, a deaf man who had worked with us at the camp for many years ran want ads in the newspaper out in Crestwood, California, asking for horses.

My friend Dale Samford once again came with his truck, and a horse trailer with an open top, and we set out for California. We made the mistake of going through Death Valley in the daytime; I have never seen such heat in my life. We got there, and the pastor of the church had a motel where he let us stay. Even the cold water was hot! We took showers with the cold water, which scalded us.

We went out to get the horses that had been donated, but were told there was no way we could haul them in the open-top trailer in the heat. They said they would all be blind before we got there. So Brother Samford bought a big goose neck trailer. He had a son who had passed away in the Los Angeles area, and we went down and picked up his car and his truck. We pulled the empty open-top trailer back with that pick-up, hooked the big goose neck to his big truck, and I drove the car back.

We were also told that we could adopt two mares with colts from the Bureau of Land Management, as they were getting on the runway of the air force base. They were wild mustangs, and we found out later that they really could not be tamed, as they were so inbred.

Anyway, we started for home and got back. We had the horses in the corral, but while we were unloading them, one of the mustangs had run into barbed wire, and had a big gash down her side. The vet said I would have to give her shots. We managed to get her tied to the barn with a gate up against her so I could give her a shot. Well, that didn't do much good. As I started to give her a shot, she kicked and carried on, and the gate between her and I disintegrated. I went flying through the air. But anyway, she healed up.

We had a plumbing problem, and I went to town to get something to see if I could fix it. While I was gone, there was a pick-up truck that had been sitting along the road watching our camp. After I left, he drove down to the corral, and the guys told me that they saw him tossing something over for one of the mustangs to eat. It was Maybelle that had eaten, and when I got back she was very, very sick. The nearest vet was nearly 150 miles away, so the farm advisor came out. Here was this mustang you couldn't get close to, lying on the ground. He gave her IV's, and we kept her covered with blankets all night, but we couldn't figure out what was wrong with her. The next morning the horse was dead, and we took her out, and buried her. We later found out it was the lawyer hired by the TV evangelist, back East.

About 7:30 that morning, here came a police car with its lights on, and TV crews from Albuquerque that had left there at 4:00 in the morning. They said they understood that we had starved a horse to death, and they wanted to see it. I said, "No we didn't starve a horse to death, but we had one that got very sick, and suspect it might have been poisoned. The farm advisor worked with it most of the night but we could not save the horse." They were upset that we had already buried the horse. They kept going on about starved horses. I said, "We've got others, please take pictures of them," but they would not.

When it came out on the news that evening, Channel 4 in Albuquerque, we couldn't watch it, but later we got a copy. It not only aired in Albuquerque, but over their satellite stations all over the state of New Mexico and into Arizona. They would ask me a question and I would answer it honestly, but then they would break in. They had gone and interviewed the woman that was living with this lawyer, though to my knowledge she had never been on the ranch, and she would say, "That blankety-blank pastor is lying to you. He is starving those horses," and went on, and on, and on. I've never understood why the TV stations would let such language be used on the air. That was the end of any churches wanting to come to camp.

We were struggling with no money, but we had a burden to reach lost souls. We had no bus, but I went to the projects all over El Paso to the managers, and said, "If you will send your kids to camp they will come back better kids. We are talking about rough gang members." They said fine. The problem was how to get them there. We had cars, and so on, but finally a man who bought buses in the United States and sold them in Mexico said he would help me out. He would loan us various buses, and we would pick up these kids and take them to camp. Often we would have two or three different gangs, and they all wanted to fight. It was really something to try and preach to a bunch of gang members. They all had some kind of weapon in their hand. If it was not a knife, it was a club, a tool, a rock, or something; they were ready to fight and defend themselves from each other.

As the week would go on, they would lay down their weapons. The Lord touched their hearts, and they would come to know Christ as Savior. Finally, by the end of the week, when it was time to go home, these rough gang members had become boys and girls who cried because they had to go back to the cities. We did this week, after week, after week and not one paid a cent.

I remember I was preaching one evening, and somebody had brought in another bus load of gang members. I finished the service, and went out and asked if they had eaten. They said, "No." We went down to the dining hall where we fixed them something to eat. I noticed that our big flood light there had burned out. I said to myself, "We need to get that fixed first thing in the morning. We don't need any dark spots."

About that time I heard them say, "Let's get the preacher." I was attacked by three guys. One of them was a big, big white boy, and he was holding one arm. A Mexican guy had the other arm, and had a knife, and had already made a slash on my arm. A black guy behind me was holding my hands. It looked like a hopeless situation, but as I mentioned earlier in the book, I grew up from the time I was six years old milking six cows every night and every morning by hand. I had my thumb and forefinger that I could use, and so I backed into one young man and pinched his tummy. He hollered out and let go of my hands. This startled the other two. I swung my arms around, and put a pinch on each of their biceps, and they fell to the ground. It is amazing what a little pinch in the right place can do. They got up, and shook themselves, and said, "I don't think we better mess with the preacher."

Another time I was surrounded by gang members, and I called them a bunch of wet-nose babies, and told them to get back to bed, and that I was the head gang member of this camp. They seemed to believe me and went off to bed. None of these paid a dime, but we were seeing lots and lots of souls saved.

Chapter 14

How Will God Pay for the Load of Food?

Well, we continued to fill the camp with gang members week after week, after week. But the money just wasn't coming in. The camp was full, it was Friday, and we had run out of groceries, but we had a semi load coming that day out of Silver City. It was a truck that made the rounds up through New Mexico over into Arizona on a two-day trip. I was praying desperately and had called El Paso to see if any money had come in, as I knew the grocery bill was going to be $1,200.00. No, no money had come in. I was on my knees in my room praying, "Lord, this is the time now that You send in someone with $1,200.00 for the grocery truck." Well, I heard someone come in, but when I went to look it was the semi load of groceries and not someone with the money. I told the boys to help unload the truck and I went back to praying.

I said, "Lord, this is Your work. We are winning these boys and girls to You, Lord. We are making decent citizens out of gang members. Lord, you have paid our bills again and again." In fact, many a time I had taken all of our bills, laid them on the altar, opened them up so God could see them and said, "Lord, this is Your work and these are Your bills. You're sure going to get a bad reputation if You don't pay Your bills." Each time, sure enough, boy, right away they would get paid.

Yes I believe that God is, but on this day nothing had happened. The truck was nearly unloaded and it seemed just as clear as a bell God said, "You do trust Me, don't you? You know I've got the check covered."

I said, "Lord I can't write a check with no money."

He said, "The check is covered." So I went down and wrote the check for the groceries for $1200.00. This is something I have never done, something I would never do on my own, but the Lord said, "Trust Me." I knew the grocery truck would not be able to take the check to the bank until Monday. I thought, "Well, when I get to El Paso, the money will have come in," and I said, "Lord, I thank You for taking care of the bill." (Don't ever try this!)

When I got home nothing had come in. I preached in church that morning about how wonderfully God had blessed and all of the souls that had been saved and the lives that had been changed that week. I didn't mention anything about the grocery bill, that was between God and I. I went home and ate a quick dinner and came back to church and I prayed, I guess you would say. I was really asking God why He had let me down. I said, "Lord, You gave me a promise and I acted on that promise. Now that check will hit the bank on Monday and there won't be any money there." I realized somebody was knocking and I went to the door and a Mexican man named Rudy was standing there.

He said, "Preacher, do you have someone in your office? I heard someone talking."

I said, "No Rudy I was just talking to God."

He came in and said, "Preacher, how was camp this week?"

I said, "Oh Rudy, it was so wonderful." I told him of all the people that had gotten saved, and how the lives had turned around. (By the way, the three gang members that attacked me at camp that week, all got saved. The last I heard, the big white boy was pastoring in the Pan Handle of Texas.) Truly God was good, and I didn't want to share the problems. I just wanted to share the wonderful things God was doing.

We had a good visit, and when he got ready to leave he pulled a small envelope out of his pocket. He said, "Preacher, some of my friends and I got together and we want to have a part in all of those people getting saved. Here is a little offering."

I said, "Thank you Rudy." I stuck it in my pocket and he went on. I didn't expect it to be more than a few dollars and didn't even count it. I went back to praying or perhaps arguing with God as to why He had not covered that check.

Suddenly the Holy Spirit smote my heart and I thought it would break. It was as if He said, "Why don't you look in your pocket?" I stopped praying, took the little envelope out of my pocket and began to count: 1, 2, 3, and on up to 12. Not $12, but 12 $100 bills.

I said, "Lord I am so sorry. I knew You would come through. Forgive me for being impatient." Monday morning the Secretary put the money in the bank and when the check arrived it was covered. Don't we have a wonderful, wonderful God? I hope He never puts you through the test as He did me that week! I wouldn't advise it to anyone, but truly God Is!

All summer long we were out rounding up people, bringing them to camp and getting them saved. We took a break one week for Mexican camp and went to a little village. In this little village a deaf girl had come to our camp and been saved. She had such a testimony that I felt a burden to go and try to reach others in that village. When I had gotten home on Saturday I had spent the day going from door to door. Most of the people did not speak English; it was just over the New Mexican boarder, at the Texas/New Mexico line. The streets were dirt and the houses were little adobe houses. I took someone with me that spoke both English and Spanish to translate, and invited them to come for a week of camp. They said they would.

We waited until Monday morning since there were no lights there, so I got to spend Sunday night at home. We had an old army bus that a bus dealer had loaned me. It was painted green and it needed a lot of work. It was one of those buses you frequently stopped and checked the diesel fuel and filled with oil. In fact it took 34 quarts of oil both ways to and from the camp. I also had a truck that Brother Samford had given me. We piled it high with luggage with the kids on the bus, as it didn't have any luggage compartments. The bus was packed, but at this one particular little house a mother said, "My little girls want to go to camp with you." They were 10 and 12, I believe. She said, "But I don't know you. I don't know where your camp is." In order for them to go, you must take my 21 year-old daughter with you."

I said, "Of course, we would love to have your 21 year-old daughter come."

We loaded the truck and bus up with luggage and went on to the camp. It was another great week, although their parents mostly spoke Spanish, the children went to school and knew English. We preached and many, many souls were saved, but I could see the 21 year-old girl was under tremendous conviction. Thursday noon I sat at her table and spoke with her. I said, "I can see you are under great conviction, wouldn't you like to accept Jesus Christ as your Savior?"

She said, "No, no I would betray my mother, and my grandmother, and my great grandmother. This is not my church." I explained to her it wasn't the church, but Jesus Christ who saved us, and she was so under conviction! Again that night she nearly held on to the pews fearing that something was going to happen to her, and again on Friday, and Friday night, but she did not get saved. Saturday morning I was busy around the camp and the bus had left. I had the luggage but I thought, "I can catch up with them before they get home." Finally it dawned on me that the bus had left, and this 21 year-old girl had not trusted Jesus Christ as her Savior. My heart was smitten. I told folks, "I've got to go, I've got to go."

I got in my truck and I raced to look for the bus. I thought surely I would find it. It ran much slower than I could go in the truck but, no, I could not find the bus.

I got to Silver City. I said, "Did someone come in here and buy some diesel fuel and oil?"

"No, we haven't seen them here." I couldn't understand. They must have gone to a different station. I rushed on and finally I got to the halfway point between the camp and El Paso. There was a little rest area beside the road that had a bathroom. We always made a stop there, so I got out and looked all through the trash to see if I could find something that looked like it had come from our snack shop. I could not find anything. I set there praying with my head in my hands. I couldn't understand how I had missed the bus.

After sitting and praying for a long time, I looked up at the 180 highway, and said, "That has to be our bus!" Sure enough, pretty soon it pulled in, and when it did and the door opened, I darted in the door down the aisle to the back of the bus. There was this 21 year-old girl. She was crying and she looked up and she said, "Pastor Lang, I am not saved." While everybody was piling off the bus to use the restroom I

sat down beside her with my Bible and led her to
Jesus Christ. My, she was so thrilled and so happy!
You see, it's important that we win everyone that we
possibly can.

Several weeks later that summer some
missionaries asked if they could bring a group out of
Old Mexico for a Spanish camp. They had gotten
permission, but something had happened to the camp
they were going to go to. I said, "Sure, we would like
to have you." Since everybody else was coming to
camp for free, why not them too? So we had camp. We
had a number of Spanish speaking pastors from El
Paso and Juarez and had a great Spanish camp. They
had not only a lot of young people but also a lot of
adults. There was one lady that sat and didn't seem
to be friends with anybody else. She would just sit in
the services and smile. She did not get saved on
Wednesday night, and Thursday I asked one of the
missionaries if he would go talk to the lady. He said,
"Sure, when I get a chance." Well something
happened and nobody got a chance.

By Friday noon, no one had talked to the lady, and
I was so burdened for her. I went to one of the tables
while we were eating and I said to a missionary,
"Come with me." We went and sat across from her at
her table, and I had him interpret for me. I said, "Do
you know Jesus Christ as Savior?"

"Oh sí, sí Señor."

I thought, "Oh yeah, you don't even know what I
am talking about."

So I asked her several different ways and I always got, "Oh sí, sí Señor."

Finally out of frustration I said, "Tell me how you got saved." I had seen so many thousands of people, I didn't realize she was from that same little Mexican village. I didn't recognize her.

She said, "Señor," and she told me how that I had come to her house and invited her children to come to camp. She said, "I didn't know you, and I asked if my 21 year-old daughter could come along."

"Oh sí, sí Señora." I remembered. She said, "My daughter told me how all week she was under conviction. The little girls got saved but she was afraid. She told me how you had chased her bus down, 150 miles, to tell her about Jesus Christ. She told me, 'Mama, Mama you must get saved too.'

I had a Spanish Bible and the young girl started looking in it but she just couldn't remember the different words from English. She said, 'Oh Mama, Mama, Pastor told me how to be saved out of the Bible, but I can't find the verses.' We were so frustrated. She said, 'Mama a family over on the other side of the village, I think they go to a Spanish Baptist Church. I believe Pastor Lang is a Baptist. Maybe they will know.'

She ran barefoot across the village to where the lady lived that went to a Spanish Baptist Church. She said, 'Can you show us out of the Spanish Bible how to accept Jesus?'

She said, 'I think I can.'

So she came back with the young lady to her Mama, and she said, 'Mama, Mama, this lady can show us out of our Bible.' So she took the Bible and showed me how to get saved that day. Oh, I am so thrilled! We all go to church with that lady now. My daughter told me you were going to be having a Spanish Camp, and I got a ride. I just had to come and meet the man who was so concerned that my children got saved, and through them I got saved. I really enjoyed the camp this week." Praise God! When we win someone to Christ, we never know how far it is going to travel.

Chapter 15

A Friend Will Stick Closer Than a Brother

I have mentioned my dear friend Brother Dale Samford from Tennessee. He and I grew up together from the time we started playing in the sandbox at the Horace Baptist Church, at age three. What a close Brother and friend he has been down through the years! Dale was then living in Murfreesboro, Tennessee, and has since moved to Manchester, Tennessee, but his business is still in Murfreesboro.

As I mentioned, a friend took me to camp I discovered that everything was gone. We got a phone put back in, and I went to try and get things arranged for camp. We had no cook, we had no help. I stopped by the food bank in Albuquerque, and they had cases and cases of cracked eggs that they wanted to give us. We had gotten another freezer at the camp, as all of our old ones had been sold. So we brought the eggs, and another man and I cracked them, and put them in plastic jars in the freezer so we could use them that summer.

157

The phone rang, and it was Mrs. Schlageter, a lady I had never met or heard from. She said, "We want to be missionaries and we have heard about your camp. Could we come and work for you?"

I said, "Well, I have an empty house and I certainly need help. Could you cook?" She said, "Yes I could do that, and my husband is a good mechanic." Jack Schlageter is probably one of the finest mechanics I have ever known. Though he is in very poor health now with diabetes and unable to work any longer, I often call him to ask how to do things. She said, "We need some way to move to the camp." Well, it turned out they weren't too far from my friend Brother Samford. I called him, and told him about the couple. He said, "You don't have any trucks anymore. I have an old International truck here with a flat bed on it, and I will donate it. You tell him to come here and get the truck. I even have a box to sit on it, that they could put their furniture in and use to move to the ranch." I called them back, and they went and picked up the truck, went back, and got all of their belongings. Brother Samford told them to stop by on their way and he would give them some gas to make the trip to the ranch.

When they pulled in, he said, "You know Pastor doesn't have a tractor anymore either, and he needs something to work the fields there." (We usually sow wheat in the fields for the horses to graze.) One of his men was out in the field baling hay. Brother Samford said to another hired man, "Go out and tell Terry to unhook that baler and drive that tractor up here." In the meantime, he told Jack to back around to a flat trailer, and he hooked it on to a truck. It had ramps on the back. Dale told Terry, "Drive that tractor up on the trailer." They need a tractor out there at the ranch".

So the tractor was loaded and tied down. Dale's baler sat in the field as he had no tractor to finish baling hay. He sent them on their way, and when he could he went out and bought another tractor and finished baling. This is a wonderful tractor, and we still use it regularly at the ranch. It has been that way over the years. Most of the vehicles, equipment, and things we have around the ranch, Dale gave to us, or talked someone else into giving us.

We were in need of a dump truck, and Dale was putting a new roof on a barn one day, and there sat an old Ryder truck that had a moving van on it. He told the man about our camp, and he said, "They could sure use that truck out at the camp. They would give you a tax receipt for it."

He said, "That sounds great. Take it." I was in Tennessee soon after this and though the van truck would be nice, I really needed a dump truck.

Dale said, "I would like to have that van body. I've got a twin cylinder dump and bed over here, I will just swap you even for them." So we took the van body off, and he put it on a trailer that he used to haul his show harness in, and Terry, one of his men painted beautiful scenes on both sides of it. It was quite a show trailer. We put the dump on the truck. Now we had a truck we could use over the road to haul things. We could use a dump truck at the camp to haul gravel out of the creek beds, to make concrete, and so on. We blew the engine a few years ago, and we got another truck, but an Indian pastor gave us an engine. We have fixed it now, and are still using it to this day.

We were really badly in need of a back hoe, but back hoes are very expensive. Jack had gone back to see his family in the dump truck, as Dale had some things he was going to donate to us once again. I had told Dale to be praying for us, that God would provide a back hoe. There was a big railroad company that had hundreds of back hoes, and had offered Dale a job. He wasn't interested in the job, but said "I have a nephew that could really do a great job." He was a very talented man, and they wanted him very badly. So he worked it out that if his nephew went to work for them, they would donate a back hoe to the ranch.

Their back hoes were fitted to work with ties, rails and so on, but they said, "Yes we will donate it, and we will even put a bucket on the back hoe." Jack was already on his way to Tennessee to see his family and to get some things. They put a trailer on the back of the truck loaded the things on it and said, "Now you go to St Joseph, Missouri, and pick up this back hoe." So off they went to Missouri, unhooked the trailer, got the big back hoe on the back of the flat bed dump, and set off for the ranch. My, what a lifesaver this has been to us down through the years! It is something we use almost constantly, with so many septic tanks and septic lines to repair, as well as water lines and crossings to fix. It is something that gets used almost all of the time.

On another occasion, we needed our big truck that

we hauled hay on, which gets three miles to the gallon, for a water truck, and we needed something more economical to haul hay. Dale was putting a roof on a house one day, of a man that had owned racehorses. He had a big International truck with a triple-nickel V8 Cummins engine in it, and a horse van body on the back. Dale said, "You know you ought to give that truck to a Christian camp out west. They could sure use that truck."

He said, "I am a Jew."

Dale said, "You still ought to give it."

He said, "Well, I am not going to." Dale said, "Well, I am going to pray you will never sell that truck, because it ought to go out there to the ranch."

Anyway he went on, and about a year later the man asked him to come out and put a new roof on his barn. Sure enough the truck was still sitting there. He said, "I see you still have the ranch's truck."

And he said, "Yes, ever since you were here not one soul has looked at that truck. I want you to take it out there, and give it to them." Well, that is exactly what happened. We took the van body off and used it for storage. We put the big 26 foot hay bed from the old truck on the big International, and now we had a powerful economical truck that we could haul hay with. There is no hay that could be grown where the ranch is, up in the mountains – not enough flat land and not enough rain. So we either have to go 125 miles to Socorro, or 200 some miles to Farmington, or 125 miles to Safford to haul our hay; and our riding horses eat a lot of hay. This truck has served us very well over the years, until last summer.

Vince usually hauls our hay, but it was a busy time, and he asked Charlie Roper to go get a load of hay. He got the nine tons of hay, and was coming up through Mule Creek Pass with it, when a sports car came around a curve straddling the center line, forcing the truck off of the side of the road. The truck lay over on its side. Thank goodness it had just come past the area where there were 1000 foot drop offs with hardly any shoulder. I had taken my wife to a doctor in Silver City, when I got the call that the truck had been turned over. I called the ranch, told them to take the box truck that we haul groceries in (which my son-in-law, Charles Aiken, had gotten the pharmaceutical company to donate to us when they closed their plant in El Paso) and two pick ups, with horse trailers, so they were able to salvage most of the hay. The fire department had come and they had managed to upright the truck, but the police had already called the wrecker service, and insisted that they had to haul the truck off. If I could have gotten there in time, I would have made arrangements with one of the ranchers to pull it off onto his field until we could get it, but the truck was hauled way off to Willcox, Arizona.

Well, we were busy in camp. All of the windows were broken out of the truck and the top was ripped off. So now it was a convertible truck in very bad shape. Willcox, Arizona is a long ways from the ranch. The first thing I did was call my friend Dale and told him what had happened. He was as sad as we were; we didn't know how we were going to haul our hay now. He called back and said, "I saw a truck up in Indiana, a 1990 Ford F 8000. It has a Fed Ex bed on it. We might pray about that." Within four or five days everything was settled. The truck dealer, with Dale putting some money down, was going to donate the rest to the camp. Our good friend, Jim Mullinex, flew to Louisville, Kentucky, where they picked him up and took him over to Indiana. He got the truck and drove it back to the ranch. The truck was specially made with steel rollers in the bottom. It had a top and back door, but the sides were open, and it had canvases that closed. It had a really nice box that was suppose to tilt, but we never figured out how it worked. Somehow you could stick a computer in and it would weigh the loads. It had a Tommy lift on the back.

Well, this was all well and good, but we just needed a plain old hay truck. We made arrangements with the people that had picked up the hay truck to pay the tow bill, and Charlie and I took the yellow dump truck and went down with a tow bar to get the truck. We hooked it up, but the big, old International is such a big, heavy truck, that towing it, our truck was stable but would sway a little bit. A policeman come to meet us, and said he had gotten a cell call that the truck was weaving. The only thing we knew was for Charlie to get back in the truck and steer it. He was squinting his eyes a lot with no windshield or top on the truck, but we started the tow back.

As we came up through Mule Creek Pass, we had to pull it in first and second gear, and going down the hills, we had to do the same. It was the only way we could hold the truck back without burning up the brakes on the dump truck. We got about ¾ of the way home when the points and coil burned from all of this low-speed driving in our dump truck. We went off and left the truck, and called Vince to come and get us. Since there is no place to get parts anywhere around where we live, on Friday I took my son to the doctor in Silver City and got the points. The men met me back there when we came back through. We got the truck fixed, and finally got it home, and switched the beds. Isn't God good!!!!

We've never had a thirteen-year-old truck before. God is so good, and so gracious, and how we love Him and thank Him for the way He provides, and for our friend who has been such a help down through the years. When everything he had given us had been sold, and was gone, he was there when we started back up again, and has helped us replenish with bigger, and better than we have ever had. God Bless you Brother Dale Samford!!!

Chapter 16

The Train

From the early days of the ranch we always had cowboy cookouts up the road, about two miles. Half of the group would ride horses up, and the other half would go on a hay wagon behind the tractor. We would go up to Whiskey Creek where there was a big turn around area, and then come back and pull off to the side of the road to our north 40. When we first started there was hardly any traffic, as the road just went to the top of the mountain and stopped, but now the road goes all the way up to Quemado and junctions in with Route 60, which goes cross-country. During the year that I was completely out, and the folks from back East ran the camp, one horse had been hit by a truck, and so we didn't feel it was safe to ride the horses now that there was traffic on the highway.

I was in room number six one night, (this was our 12 x 16 home at the ranch for 20 some years) and I was having severe chest pains. Well, the worst thing to do when you are trying to have a heart attack is lay there and let it happen. So I decided to get up and start something new. It has always been amazing to me that men will work all of their life, retire, and sit down and watch television, and die usually within six months to two years. There is something between the brain and the heart, and when the brain says to the heart, "I don't think you're needed anymore," it just ups and quits.

So I got up, went to my desk in the corner, and said, "I am going to start something new." I prayed about it, got out some paper, and begin to draw. I drew a train that looked like an old steam engine with cars behind it. I worked feverishly until breakfast time, and when I went to the camp breakfast I told Jack Schlageter the family living there at the time. I said, "Jack we are going to build a train."

He said, "I know you have lost your mind." Jack was an excellent welder. Once I got the vision for building the train, everywhere I went I was looking for something to build it with.

Right after that, one of the men in the church said, "Preacher would you have any use for an old GMC truck?" My brother in-law left it here. He lost the title, and it doesn't have an engine, and the transmission is out, but if you have any use for it you can have it.

I said, "Thank you, that is exactly what I need." I loaded it on the back of a trailer behind our '69 Ford truck, and it was in that trip that we stopped at the little Mexican village and picked the folks up on an old army bus.

Just as I went to turn back onto the highway, the steering wheel began to spin, but the wheels did not turn. The old cab had settled down on the frame, and apparently had been resting on the steering column and cut it in half. Was I ever glad that it happened there, and not when I was going through the mountains, where I would have had no control at all! Obviously, that truck would have to stay put until I could come back, go to a junk yard, and get a new steering shaft from the steering wheel to the gear box. Eventually, we got the old truck to the ranch, took the cab off, took the bed off, and then we had a ¾ ton running gear. I had to get another truck to haul the luggage.

A short time later I was in Tennessee, and I went to Young's junk yard and asked him if he had a 192 straight six GMC engine. He said he did, and he would gladly donate it. We put it in, buckled up the transmission, (after the train was built we had to take it out and have it rebuilt) and now we had a running gear. With it stretched out long, the steering wheel had to come back where the truck bed would have been, and there was no room for a radiator, so we had to put in a different radiator with an electric fan. I was at an auction, and they had a great big LP gas tank that somebody had cut a hole in the top of, and they were using it for a water wagon. I bought it real cheap and brought it back. We cut a hole in the front of it, cut the back side off, cut the bottom out, and fit it on the train. John Coons, one of our board members in El Paso had some old signs that were made out of granite, and they had a few holes in them where the neon lights had gone, but they looked just perfect. It looked like we had train robbers and the train had been shot up. We put these on, made the coal car, built a frame, put the top back over the engineer's compartment, and put a bow roof on it.

Then one day I was visiting Ed Blakeslee, who had been a missionary in Brazil for 25 years on the Amazon, but now had a branch church off of our church to the Spanish speaking people of El Paso. He was showing me a new long horn bull that he had, and as we walked along I said, "Ed why do you have the smoke stack of our train laying here in the fence row?" It was a big, round pipe just the right height.

He said "I am not even going to ask what you are talking about, just go put it in your truck." So the engine was coming together.

While I was in Tennessee, I got the engine. My friend Dale Samford had the neatest little wagon. I said, "Dale, where did you get that wagon?"

He said, "My brother William bought 65 of these when Eastern Airlines went bankrupt. Maybe he would give you some."

I called William, and he said, "I'm sorry I can't give you any, but you could buy them for $1500 a piece." Well, we didn't have $1500. I told him I would pray for him, in case somewhere along the line he would decide to tithe some of them.

I went on back to El Paso, and it wasn't long until we were sending our old yellow dump truck back to pick up a load of stuff that Dale had donated to us. Jack Schlageter was driving the truck. I got a telephone call at the ranch from William Samford. He said, "Preacher I haven't been able to sleep. I believe I could tithe three of those Eastern Airline baggage cars."

I said, "The truck is on the way, it should be there today or tomorrow". Well, that surprised him as he was down in Georgia, but they were able to put two of the wagons on the back of the truck, and pull another behind, and still load a lot of the stuff on that truck that Dale had gotten for us.

Now that we had the airline baggage carts we went to work on them. I had Jack weld an extension 16 inches wide on both sides and on each end, making the cars bigger. Then we made a metal frame, and got wood and build the railroad cars and the seats inside. By the time camp started we had a train for our cowboy cookout. It really looks quite authentic. From JC Whitney I got what they called an old steam engine train whistle. I put a cassette player in, and a speaker, and as the train goes down the road you can hear it going, "chugga, chugga, chugga chugga." You can also hear the clickity clack of the tracks, the ding dong of the bell, and ever so often the blowing of the steam whistle. It sounds just like the real thing.

It is such a nice looking train. Every year the county would ask us to bring it and drive it in the 4th of July parade. Two or three years we took it to the Pie Town Festival in Pie Town, but the 60 mile trip one way was a bit much.

Each morning we have devotions in the chapel at 7:30, then we go to the flag pole, say the pledges, and line up at the dining hall for breakfast at 8:00. As soon as they come out of chapel, the ones that are going on the cowboy cookout that day load on the train. We have one each day until everyone gets to go.

This canyon used to be a robbers' roost, where the Butch Cassidy gang, Billy the Kid and others lived. It seems there are always still some robbers up in the hills, so Sheriff Rainbow Bill always rides the train to protect us. Sure enough, when we get to the turn around, somebody will come asking for help, and lead the Sheriff off in the wrong direction while the outlaws sneak up and rob the train. Well, Rainbow Bill always comes back, and the outlaws meet their demise. Then we turn around, and go back down the road a little ways and park beside our north 40. My, what a string of kids you see going down the hillside, and wonder how they all fit on the train, usually 50 to 60 kids. Besides the two car loads, (the engine didn't have enough power to pull three), we have bus seats in the coal car, and so it really carries a big load.

Once we get down to the cowboy cookout, there are logs that beavers had cut that we use for benches, and over an open fire the wrangler is busy cooking pancakes, bacon, and eggs. Young people line up, get a pie pan, which we call a gold panning pan, and get their food. As long as they can eat, they keep cooking, and there have even been known to be flying pancakes from the grill over to where the kids are holding up their plates for seconds.

When everybody is full, and can hold no more, they go down to the creek where they get some gravel and water, swirl it around, and pan for gold. A few have found some gold flakes. One lady, who was very critical of the camp, found a large gold nugget. Well, the Lord put her in her place, and that was the end of her complaining about our gold panning experience. They don't always find gold, but they always get the syrup off, so the pie pans don't stick together on the way back to the kitchen. It is a lot of fun, and everybody really enjoys it, eating like the cowboys did over a fire.

It is the first and only train that has ever been in Catron County. This is just some of the many things that make camp so exciting for the young people. For many of the inner city kids, who have never been out of the large cities, and away from their projects, this is the most exciting thing they have ever seen.

APACHE CREEK LIMITED

Pastor Lang at 3 a.m. with chest pains had a vision and draws out plans for a train for the camp which he and Jack had ready for summer camp. Here they are on their way to the Cowboy Cookout.

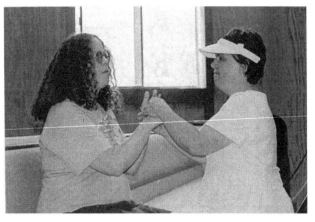

Both these ladies are deaf, the one on the right is also blind.

Chapter 17

Deaf Camps

In the beginning, I told you how I became burdened for the deaf and all the measures I went to to try to reach the deaf in the western United States. After these many years, there are many deaf spread around the world that came to know Jesus Christ, and received their training at Apache Creek Deaf and Youth Ranch. The wife of the deaf pastor, and the head of the deaf school at First Baptist Church, Hammond, found Christ at our camp. Missionaries serving in Cuba, the Philippines, Guyana and in many other countries got their burden for working with the deaf from our camp, and we could go on, and on, and on.

Many people really do not understand the deaf. They used to be called the deaf and dumb; deaf because they could not hear, and dumb because they could not speak. The deaf are very intelligent, as much so as anybody, and in many ways have sharpened abilities that others don't have. Many deaf work in post offices, because their hand and eyes are so quick. Many others work in print shops, and various places.

Deafness doesn't affect anything except that they are unable to hear and therefore unable to learn in a hearing society. For example, a hearing child entering school knows 5,000 words. He can't spell them, he can't read them, but when he hears them, he knows what they mean because he has been hearing them every day, and associating those words with things. It is not so with a deaf child. In fact, a deaf person who has gone through years of schooling is fortunate to learn 800 words. You see, deaf people do not think in words and sentences as the hearing person does. Their language is a picture language, and they think in pictures. They are usually very blunt, and their sign names for people are a picture of what they see in them. We used to have a man in our church, and their sign for him was "dirty pig." He didn't take a bath very often, and didn't wash his clothes very often. They didn't mean to be unkind, that is just what they saw.

Allen Snare was our deaf pastor for a number of years. He came from Pennsylvania, and needed to get a Texas drivers' license, as I was pastoring in El Paso, Texas. He took the test twice and failed it. It so happened that the man who was giving the test to him also had his daughter in our Christian Day Care Center. My wife was talking to him, and he said he was sorry that Allen couldn't pass the written test. My wife asked him if it would be alright if she came with him the next time, and signed the test to him. He said yes he would permit that. Allen got a perfect score. You see, he just was not familiar with many of the words on the exam, but when he saw the sign for them, he of course knew exactly what they were. He was a very good driver, and was happy to get his Texas drivers' license.

As I mentioned, Allen Snare was our deaf pastor for a number of years, until we introduced him to a young lady from Colorado Springs at camp one summer. They fell in love, got married, and she wanted to stay in Colorado Springs, so he moved there to become the deaf pastor. Later he went back to Pennsylvania, and now is in the south eastern United States working with Dr Ted Camp.

We teach sign language at our camp the third and fourth week of May each year. We also have teams that go out and teach sign language all over the country, that are associated with our camp.

Our son, Craig, goes to South America, and teaches sign language. He teaches ASL, MSL, and BSL. Whatever it might be, it is primarily geared for hearing people to see inside the deaf world, and to learn their language. Deaf children go to schools where they are primarily given hearing text books, in which they do not understand most of the words, and struggle a great deal in trying to learn. Some do better than others, but it is a real struggle.

My good friend Dr Victor Vodounou was born on a jungle trail in Africa, as his mother could not make it home before he was born. He is one of the most brilliant men I think I have ever met. A French missionary ran across him as a little boy, and realized how intelligent Victor was. He taught him sign language, and what he could in Africa, and then took him to France where he put him in school. Victor knows about five different languages including his home language: French, English, Spanish, and I believe there is one other. Victor went on to go to Canada to study in college, and from there he went to New York to study, and then he went to Los Angeles and studied. One day I met him at a bus station in El Paso, Texas. He had enrolled in the University of Texas at El Paso, and during that time became the deaf pastor in our church. He finally went to Southern New Mexico University, where he received his doctorate degree. He is an absolutely brilliant man, and needs very desperately some support so he can return to Africa and build schools all over that continent to reach the deaf. He would also like to build camps there.

My burden for the deaf, and their inability to read, or think in the hearing language, was always with me. After visiting many deaf schools I was concerned that they shouldn't be given hearing books, unless they were taught to read them. For many years I thought, and thought about this, and came up with a way that I thought we could teach the deaf themselves, not only sign language but the words in the hearing language. To me it seems very simple: you would have the word, you would have the sign, you would have the picture, if it was something that there could be a picture of. In other words, you would have the word "cat," you would have the sign pulling the whiskers, and you would have a picture of the cat.

I tried and tried to get others interested in this, and finally after many years Dr. John Peterson in Brazil and Dr. Don Cabbage decided to try, and it has worked marvelously. Dr. Peterson is the one that primarily produces this, and now we have books in English, Portuguese, Spanish, and other languages around the world. We can go into a country, find deaf, video them speaking in their sign language, then match it to pictures and put the sign for their language with the picture of the subject. I would like to see this greatly expanded, and believe that we could make word building books starting with first grade, and teach perhaps a thousand words a year. Wouldn't that be something, instead of graduating from high school knowing 800 words they could know 12,000 words!

Eighty percent of all people who are called into full-time Gospel work are called at Christian Camps such as ours, and this is also true of the deaf. I remember when Pastor Mike Langin first drove all the way from Houston, Texas to our camp, and how God touched his heart and called him into the Lord's work. He went to deaf college in Illinois, ended up marrying his teacher, and for many years has been a deaf pastor in Phoenix, Arizona. What a thrill it is to see ourselves reproduced over, and over, and over again.

Our youngest son, Craig, was not even born when we started the Apache Creek Deaf and Youth Ranch. Thus he grew up from the time he was a baby in the work, and has known it all of his life. He is now our camp director and he and his wife, Debbie, are both excellent signers. They now have a little girl Rebekah who at this time is three, a son James who is two, and a daughter Bethany who was born in April. Rebekah is already using perhaps more sign language than she is using words. Though Craig, Debbie, and their children are hearing, he has a feel for the deaf. He is now our camp director at the camp, and conducts our international camps throughout South America. He has invitations to go to Cambodia, Thailand and Africa, and there are many other places which he would like to go. It is just so difficult for us to raise the funds for the airfares, and the bus tickets once he gets to these countries. For many years, he spent January and February in South America teaching Brazilian sign language, holding camps for the deaf, and sometimes camps for the street children, as he has gotten the burden for our inner city camps. He also has gone to Venezuela, Guyana, and Trinidad.

Four years ago while in Guyana, Craig found out that there was very little work being done among the deaf, and asked the minister of education at the federal level if he could come and teach the school teachers, which he did. A large number of school teachers came and learned sign language. In Guyana they speak English, so he taught them the English sign language there. He left them books, and they are on their way to starting deaf education there.

Many deaf came to the meeting because they wanted to learn how to speak to one another. There was one man who knew sign language and rounded them up. You see, still in many, countries, and sometimes in the United States, there are people who are deaf that do not know how to communicate to one another. Sign language is a language that they developed among themselves when they went to deaf schools. In fact, when we started the camp most deaf schools would not permit deaf to use sign language. What a tragic mistake! They thought they could learn to lip read and read, but they didn't know the words, and so for most it was an utter failure. You see, deaf people need someone to help them bridge the gap between them and the hearing world.

As a boy I was privileged to hear Helen Keller come and speak at the Paris High School in Paris, Illinois. She was an elderly lady at the time, and what a remarkable lady! Helen was deaf from birth. She was a very smart and intelligent girl. She was not only deaf but she was blind, and she wanted to break out of that shell. She became a holy terror to her family, and they did not know what to do with her. Finally they hired a young girl by the name of Annie Sullivan just to come and take care of her.

Annie realized what was going on with Helen, and she was determined that she was going to find a way to help her break out of that deaf and blind world that she was in. Helen could not hear nor see Annie. So Annie thought and thought. She had Helen put her fingers upon her lips and her voice box, and try to imitate her. Then she would hold her voice box, and after hours, and hours, and hours of practice, Helen Keller not only learned sign language, but learned to speak. This is one of the most remarkable cases in all of history. Had it not been for Annie Sullivan, Helen's life would have been an utter disaster. Annie devoted the rest of her life to helping Helen.

Craig left before camp was over and went to Guyana. He found out that there was a coup in the country and had trouble getting in. He finally came in on a plane with the president, which wasn't the safest place since there was a coup against him. Craig found out that the school buildings were closed. So he got a missionary to open his church to the teachers, and they came and learned. The deaf came to learn. They learned very quickly, because of our new sign language book. Before he left, he and Ed Kollmeyer, who he had brought along, held a deaf revival, and saw 30 deaf adults come to know Christ as Savior.

He trained the missionary, and left books with him to continue to train these deaf. All of a sudden the missionary had more deaf in his church than he did hearing, which made him rather nervous. These deaf, over the past four years, have not only learned more and more but are spreading out, and are teaching more deaf all over Guyana and surrounding countries. My, what a thrill it is to be able to learn to communicate, and to know Jesus Christ as Savior and to be able to communicate Him to others. So the Gospel spreads. These missionaries came to our camp for sign language this summer to learn more, and are still training the deaf there. The schools there now teach the deaf.

Yes we do have a number of deaf and blind who come to Apache Creek Deaf and Youth Ranch. We sit them in front facing the other deaf people, with their backs to the platform, and the deaf people on the front row take turns interpreting back to them what they see from the platform. You wonder how they can do this? Well, they hold the hands of the seeing deaf person, and thus they learn. What a miracle it has been to watch them over the years as they sit there with this blank face, and suddenly you see a light come on, and they begin to understand. We have deaf show up at our camps from many different countries.

Through the internet the world knows what is going on. I remember one year at camp we started counting, and we had deaf there from five different nations. We often bring a number of deaf from Mexico for our deaf camps. While one is signing in American Sign Language, someone that knows American and Mexican sign language will interpret from the American to the Mexican sign language for those who are there. What a marvelous opportunity to spread the Gospel to so many that would never otherwise have an opportunity to hear. Craig also preaches each year at a large deaf fellowship in Mexico. As the Bible told thousands of years ago, *"And in that day shall the deaf hear the words of the book."* (Isaiah 29:18). It is so humbling to realize that we are playing a major role in doing that here at the Apache Creek Deaf and Youth Ranch, and our son and his wife as they travel across the country and around the world to take the Gospel to those who have never had an opportunity.

Craig and Debbie are trying now to raise money to go to Madagascar (a large island east of Africa). The Pritchards, missionaries there, came to our camp to learn sign language and worked the rest of the summer at our camp to catch the spirit of the camp. We always have to pray in the funds for these trips.

They are trusting God that they will be able to set up a deaf school there by September or October 2006. If you can help with this or other trips please contact us.

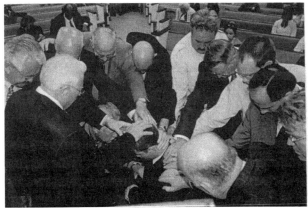

Dr. Dean Lang at Pastor Craig Lang's ordination.

Pastor Lang surveying building projects on his buckskin mare. First building used as a kitchen in the beginning. The building on the right is a bath house. The cabins in the back are dorms.

Chapter 18

Inner-City Camp

Over the years there have been thousands that have come to our Inner City Camps. In El Paso, Texas, one of the large gangs is called the Fatherless Gang, and perhaps this is true of many of the inner city children. People often wonder why they form gangs. First of all, they form gangs to become part of their family, and to protect themselves from other gangs, but then they usually get carried away and involved in some unbelievable crimes. It is especially horrible what the girls have to go through to get into these gangs, and for many of them it seems almost impossible to get out. By the grace of God many of them do get out of the gangs.

I remember one inner city camp in particular, a very clean-cut, nice-looking young man came to me, and said, "Pastor Lang, do you remember me?"

So many have gone through our camp! I looked at him, and something was familiar, but I couldn't place him. I said "I'm not sure, but I don't believe this is the camp you belong in."

He said, "Oh I looked just like the rest of them last year. You led me to Christ, and told me to go home, get out of the gang, find a church and get into it. When I got home I looked around, and two blocks from my house there was a Baptist Church. I went Sunday morning, and told them that I had been saved at your camp, and wanted to be baptized. "One by one I began to win my sisters to the Lord, and then my brothers, and then finally my mother. It's been a year, and we finally won my father to the Lord, and he was baptized last Sunday. God has called me to be a preacher, and after I finish this last year of high school I am going to Bible school to prepare for the ministry." My, what might his life had been like, had he not come to camp!

Another young man came to camp, and was greatly under conviction, but the gang members had told him, "If you go to that camp, and get saved we are going to kill you." He resisted until Friday evening, then trusted Christ as his Savior. We were having a testimony meeting around the bonfire, and he gave his testimony, and told how he had been threatened.

He said, "I have decided that I would rather have Jesus. If they kill me, I know I will go to Heaven." His mother did not have a phone, and I couldn't call her. I believed the threat against his life was very real. When I stopped the bus, in El Paso, TX., and she came to pick him up, I told her about what had happened. I said that I would be glad to take him back to the camp and let him live with us until something could be worked out. She was very worried, but said, "Let me wash up his clothes, and I will find somebody to bring us back up."

Well they didn't come, and we found out that not only he but his little brother had disappeared right away. The mother was very distraught, and everyone assumed that their bodies would be found out in the desert sooner or later. Three months went by, and one day he walked into the house and said, "Mama we can't hide out any longer." She got some help, took both boys to the airport and flew them to Puerto Rico where his father lived. He told her that they had told him they were not only going to kill him, but his little brother, and he had to protect him. How Satan puts up a fight to keep them, but God gives the victory!

Many have come to our camp, have gotten saved instead of dropping out of school, and have gone on to high school, even to college, and have become very productive citizens.

A young girl who came to our camp (I will not go into to all of her story), came back a few years later with four or five children and her husband, and said, "Pastor Lang my husband is going to church with me, but he doesn't understand how he can know for sure he is going to heaven. I knew if I could get him here that you could win him to the Lord." They helped us with inner city camp that week and he was among the first to put his faith, and trust in Jesus Christ. The mother also had come, and got up and gave a testimony of how ashamed she was that she had tried everything to derail her daughter, but her daughter had stayed faithful, and went to church, and she had gotten saved and went to church with her every week. Yes, there is a God in Heaven that loves and cares for inner city children.

I could tell you hair-raising stories, but the story I would rather tell is how after a week at camp, they become boys and girls once again, just like other children. They just needed someone to love them, someone to show them the way, someone to tell them that they could stay in school, go to college, and be productive citizens, and they do.

Chapter 19

Indian Camp

For many years we have invited the Indians to camp. If they have twenty dollars they can pay twenty dollars, if they don't have anything they can come for free as most do. We have a number of Indian reservations around us: the large Navajo reservations, the Pueblos, the Apaches, the Zunis, and the list go on and on. These are the folks that came across the Bering Straight before the rest of us. They had all come from the Tower of Babel when the languages were changed, so they knew there was a God, and they knew there was a devil, but they hadn't heard about the Lord Jesus Christ.

The Navajos didn't have a written language until 1967 when some translators made one for them. Many still can not read it, and I fear that many of the children who now go to government schools are eventually going to lose their native tongue, which will be a shame. An Indian pastor friend of mine had a brother who wanted to go back and trace his roots. He went back to Mongolia, in the mountains of China.

When he got there, the first question was, "Why have you been gone so long?" They still spoke the same Navajo language which he spoke.

I have asked the Navajos many times to tell me their stories. Since they did not have books, the grandfather and father would tell the stories to each generation and keep them alive. One day, I asked, "How far back do your stories go?" They go back to where we were in this dark place with a lot of animals; of course it would have been on Noah's Ark. Perhaps in their storytelling they kept history straighter than many who have written books.

We have had so many remarkable things happen at Indian Camp, and it is usually one of our largest camps. I remember one year there was a little girl who was so bashful. She was probably about 12 years old, and I could see the Lord was speaking to her heart, but she was so bashful. It reminded me of myself when I was nine years old and so bashful. When company would come to our house I would run and hide under the bed. I remember during a revival meeting the Lord was speaking to my heart, but I was so bashful that I was afraid to go forward. My friend Dale Samford sitting beside me leaned over and said, "Ain't you ever going to get saved?" I determined I wasn't going to be lost because I was bashful.

It was Friday afternoon and I saw the little girl sitting on a bench in front of the motel. I sat down there and asked her, "You are bashful aren't you?" She looked down, as always and she nodded her head yes. I said, "I used to be very bashful too," and I told her about it.

She looked up in surprise, "You were bashful?"

"Yes I was." I told her about how I got saved and asked her, if that is what she would like to do.

She said, "Oh yes I have just been too bashful." I led her to Christ.

Several months later I was preaching at a preachers' meeting in Phoenix, Arizona. The pastor who had brought her, Pastor Begay, and another neighboring pastor, Pastor Calvin, said to me after I preached one day, "Preacher, you know that little bashful girl you led to the Lord at camp?"

I said, "Oh yes, how is she doing? "

They said, "She is not bashful anymore." They said she went home and started talking to her brothers and sisters, and got them to come to Brother Begay's church, and finally her parents, her uncles, her aunts, her cousins and grand-parents. They said so far she has brought 27 who have trusted Christ as their Savior. Yes, God cares, and thank God somebody cared about a little Indian girl who was bashful.

A couple of years ago we had an especially large number of Indians that had not been in church and were not saved when they came to camp. Many of the Indian churches had gone out and rounded them up. I preached on Wednesday night, gave the invitation, and they came, and they came, and they came. More than 100 came, trusting Jesus Christ as their Savior. My, what an evening!

The next morning, since I am the train engineer, I was getting ready to pull out with another load for the cowboy cookout, (though the Indians sometimes call it the Indian cookout), when this teenage girl came up to the train and said, "Pastor Lang I have been waiting six months for a dentist appointment, and I have to be in Grants this afternoon. If I am not there I will lose the appointment. My tooth hurts so bad, and it might be another six months before I could get in."

I said, "Alright, pack your stuff. When I come back I will get my wife and we will take you home" (a 250 mile round trip). As I was driving the train I thought, "Brother Sarracino went up to preach in his church last night, I wondered why she didn't ride with him, and save me this long trip," but I didn't say anything.

When I came back, I got my wife, picked the girl up, and took her home. As we were driving along she was sitting in the back seat reading her Bible. Anybody that comes to our camp without a Bible, we give them a brand new King James Bible. We have given away thousands and thousands of them over the years. She said, "You know Pastor, I knew about this appointment, and I knew Brother Sarracino was coming back last night, and I thought about asking him if I could go back with him, but I was not saved, and I was afraid that if I went back I might not ever get saved. My mother is a Christian and my father and I have made it so hard for her, as we have battled against her for being a Christian. God was speaking to my heart, and I got saved last night. Now I am going to go home, and my mother and I will start working on my father, and I am sure we will be able to win him to the Lord too." The rest of the trip she would read awhile, and ask questions, and as she had answers, she went through the Bible. She was so eager to learn, and so eager to go home. She asked us to pray for her father's salvation when we dropped her off.

When we got back that night, we prayed for her father. Pastor Anna, an Indian Pastor from Oklahoma, was preaching on the need for Indians to give their lives to serve the Lord. I believe I have mentioned before that 80 percent of all the people that are called into full-time Gospel work are called at camps like this. He gave an invitation for young men who felt that God was calling them into the ministry to come. They started coming. The first young man came up, walked right up on the platform to the microphone and said, "Pastor Anna, God has called me to preach, and I think he wants me start right now." Well, he preached about a five-minute sermon, and they were still coming, and others begin to line up. They were forming long lines. Each would step up, preach a brief message, saying that God had called them to preach and to go back to the Indian nations and spread the Gospel.

Then I noticed on the other side there was a long line of girls that were lining up, and I said, "Do you girls want to say something?"

"No, we are just coming to let the Lord know that we would like to be the wives of these preachers, and help them take the Gospel." My, the service went on and on! I guess it would have gone all night. Finally at about two o'clock in the morning, I said, "We're going to have to stop for now and continue tomorrow." My how God blesses, and works in hearts and calls lives to spread His Gospel around the world!

Chapter 20

The Mountain Children

Every year we send out thousands of letters with a seventy-five dollar gift certificate for camp to every box holder that lives [within a hundred mile circle around us] to the Arizona line. Many people live back in the mountains, and may only check their mail every few months, but when they check, there is a letter from us with a gift certificate, which means instead of ninety-five dollars for camp, their children can come for twenty dollars. This is a poor area; the saw mills have been shut down by the environmentalists and the cattle industry is being greatly curtailed. So we want to do our part to help. Of course we mention in the letter if they don't have the $20, they can come for free, and many do.

I remember one year a lady called. She had gone to Glenwood about 60 miles away where she had a post office box and had the letter. She said, "I have three children, could all three of them come for twenty dollars?"

We said, "Of course they can." They came, and I remember that on Wednesday night all three of them trusted Christ as their Savior.

The next morning I walked into the dining hall and this little girl, maybe 12 years old, was jumping up and down, and came running and said, "Oh Pastor Lang, Pastor Lang, Pastor Lang, this is the bestest, bestest, bestest, bestest week of my whole life, and the bestest, bestest, bestest bestest part of all, I now have Jesus in my heart!" Oh, we've heard this again and again and again.

There is no one that is kept from coming to our camp because they don't have money. Yes, we usually end the season around $10,000 in the red, or more, and we have to pray and pray for God to supply so we can pay the bills, but it is God's work and He does meet the needs; we just trust Him.

> *But without faith it is impossible to please Him: for he that cometh to God must believe that He Is, and that He is a rewarder of them who diligently seek Him.*
>
> (Hebrews 11:6)

> *Where there is no vision the people perish.*
>
> (Proverbs 29:18)

I look out across the vast mountain ranges and I never know when I start down an old logging road, I might go 50 miles, maybe even 100 miles, and come to a ranch. Many of the ranches run cattle on a 100 sections or more, which would be a 100 square miles or more, but God loves those children who are back in the hills, whose parents teach them at home, who seldom see anyone. Yes, God loves them, and so do we.

Chapter 21

Our Church Camps

We also have a number of camps throughout the summer, where church groups bring their kids to camp. I often urge them not only to bring the kids that have money, but if they have bus kids to please bring them; nobody will know whether they paid or not. I also ask them if they can go out and have their kids bring an unsaved friend to camp with them. If the parents can pay, or the church can pay, fine; if not, we will.

Many churches have built their churches by bringing unsaved kids to camp who get saved. They have spent a week with other Christians kids and usually the pastor, or maybe the youth director, and when they go home it is easy to get them into their church because they already know them. Soon the parents are happy that somebody cares about their kids. I think most parents today are concerned about what's happening to their teenagers, and when they find somebody that cares about them they want to go to that church too. Only eternity will show how many have gotten saved through this type of ministry.

Many of the church kids have grown up in Christian homes, and thought they were saved, but when they are away from everything for a week and the Lord is dealing with their hearts, many of them find out what it truly is to be saved. Many Christian young people today have so many strong pulls from the world that it is easy for them to be pulled astray. So often Christian young people, even preachers' kids, get walkmans and start listening to rock music, and soon it has poisoned their souls. Most rock music is about drugs, immorality, and rebellion against parents. Some heavy metal music deals with Satanism and devil worship, and it's easy even for Christian kids to listen to this, and to poison their soul. Pastors and youth directors who come are encouraged to stand firm and strong, and it will strengthen many of the churches throughout our part of the country.

I thank God for the churches that bring kids to our camp. Many of them pay, and it really helps us to get through those weeks, as well as the others. All of our staff are volunteers, and are dependent upon God for missions support to meet their needs. So everything that comes in goes to reaching kids. Sometimes we even have churches that come from back east for a week, and God has done some remarkable things for these groups. They have gone back to their churches, and sometimes pastors will call and say, "What have you done to my kids?"

"Is something wrong?"

"Oh no, nothing is wrong. They came home, and brought a spirit of revival back to our church, praise God. They said they want to go out soul winning, and they are bringing new people into the church." Well, praise God for that.

We have two family camps each summer: Spanish camp on the 4th of July week, so people don't have to take quite so much time off work, and English speaking camp the second week of August. These are always great camps, usually made up with Christian people, though we do see some saved during these weeks. It is a time when pastors and church members come to hear great preaching and music. We have some wonderful times at these camps.

At these camps, many preachers, missionaries, evangelists, church families and so on come and get their batteries recharged and fired up, and it is always such a time of great revival. My, our God is so good, and we try in every way we possibly can to reach as many people as we possibly can. Did not Jesus say, "Go ye into all the world, and preach the Gospel to every creature" (Mark 16:15)?

Chapter 22

A Vision From Cross Mountain

Our camp sits in a deep canyon with high mountains on either side. To the west of the camp is Goat Mountain, which is an easy mountain to climb. Across the road is Cross Mountain, which is a very high climb, but most of our campers like to take a trip up there every Thursday afternoon. You can see mountain ranges as far as the eye can see. Down in the camp in front of the old cabin that was there when I bought the ranch is an old elm tree. I talked to a lady one day who said she and her father planted that tree when she was a little girl. The tree has had twisters twist the top out and many limbs have broken out, but the tree is over 75 feet across. In fact, it sits beside our gym that is 75 feet long, and its branches reach out past that. Under it we have a number of picnic tables. People can sit under the shade of the tree and visit or work on whatever it might be. Also, at the edge of it we have a place for the bonfire, where we often gather towards the end of the week and have testimony time.

In my vision I am standing up on Cross Mountain, and looking down into the valley. I can see people groping their way down the valley. At a closer look, I realize they are blind, they cannot see. They do not realize that they are marching towards a great chasm, a great chasm that drops into Hell. Oh, my heart is broken. Who would turn these away? I look down, and under the big elm tree I see the church gathered. Oh, they are so happy. They are sitting at the picnic tables, and at a closer look I realize they are making dandelion chains. I remember when I was two or three years old, I would go out in the yard and pick the dandelion stems, blow the fuzzy ball off, break off the tip, bring it around, stick the small end into the big end, and I would make large chains. What are they good for? Well, nothing!

But as I look down there sits the church and they are ever so busy. They are working so earnestly making dandelion chains. From the top of Cross Mountain I cried down, "Oh Church, oh Church, oh Church, can't you see the valley is full of blind people? They are marching headlong to their destruction. You all need to stretch out across the canyon and tell them to stop, tell them to look up to Jesus, that their eyes might be open. For the Bible says that Satan hath blinded the minds of them lest they should see. There is urgency-quickly, quickly, fan out across the canyon before they march to their destruction."

The church cried back, "Oh we would love to do that, Pastor, but you see we are very, very busy making dandelion chains."

I cry back, "No, forget the dandelion chains. Stretch out across the canyon and tell the blind to turn before it is too late."

"No, we are to busy making dandelion chains."

I wonder, if we take stock of our churches, how much of our effort is actually turning the blind to the Lord Jesus Christ, who can open their eyes spiritually that they might be saved and not go into destruction; or how much of it is something that we are so busy with, so important that it misses the main point. Something to think about, isn't it?

Picture taken from top of Cross Mountain.

We've been stretched across this canyon for more than 30 years and have seen in the neighborhood of ten thousand people turned unto the Lord Jesus Christ and gone to serve Him.

Chapter 23

Would You Like to Share in These Rewards in Heaven?

Paul, in writing to the church in Philippi, says, "Not because I desire a gift: but I desire fruit that may abound to your account." Yes, many have helped us as partners in changing tens of thousands of lives over these past 30 years. You can be a shining star by giving and praying to help turn these lives to serve God.

> *And they that be wise shall shine as the brightness of the firmament, and they that turn many to righteousness as the stars for ever and ever.*
>
> (Daniel 12:3)

When I think of all of the kids who have come to camp over the years who were on the wrong track, many gang members, etc., and how God changed their lives so completely, I am reminded of James 5:20.

> *Let him know, that he which converteth the sinner from error of his way shall save a soul from death, and shall hide a multitude of sins!*

We started with $5 and a handshake. We never made any great fanfare. My family and I just worked hard and sacrificed, because we wanted to help these kids. Over the last 30 years many other families have come and joined us. We are all missionaries and trust God to care for us. Everything goes to reaching the kids unless it is designated for one of the missionary families. We have maybe 100 families that give to the work from time to time, and a few churches. No one is turned away. This summer we ended camp over $17,000 in the red, but praise God, as of this day, October 24, 2005, God has paid this off. Isn't God good!!!

I'd like to be able to take better care of our faithful workers. We need to build more buildings so we can bring more to camp. My wife and I lived in a 12 x 16 room here at the camp for more than 20 years before my parents left us money to build a house. We were happy to do without, that we might help others, but I am 70 years old and I hate to leave my son and his wife with financial burdens that my wife and I have endured these 30 years. Not only that, but we are at a point where we can help so many more now, and you could share in the great rewards forever in eternity.

With the high cost of energy now, we are going to be forced to revise our fee for those with funds to $100, and also for those who can sponsor a boy or girl to camp. Just think, for $100 you could change a child's future from gangs to productive citizenship. One hundred dollars could mean that they will get saved (most do) and spend all eternity in Heaven. You could see a boy or girl called into the ministry, maybe as a

missionary that would win thousan   Lord
Jesus Christ, or a pastor and wife   win
multitudes to the Lord. We are rea   of
monthly support to pay our utility bill, fe   es,
and pay normal operating expenses. Ou   ls
missionary support. We need large g.   l
buildings, and the great part is by doing
share the rewards in Heaven. No man ever
than when he stooped to lift up a child! 1
There are two ways you can give:

Send your offering to:

Apache Creek Deaf and Youth Ranch.
P.O. Box 260
Reserve, NM 87830
Email: apachecreek@gilanet.com
Visit our website at: www.apachecreek.us

Or Call 1-800-869-0962 or 1-505-533-6969

☐ VISA   ☐ MASTERCARD

Card Number

_____

Signature_____

Exp. Date_____

Pastor Lang, here is my gift of:

☐$100.00   ☐ $200.00   ☐$500.00

☐ $_____

Pastor Lang, here is my gift for much-needed new buildings:

☐ $1,000   ☐ $5,000   ☐ $10,000
☐ $25,000   ☐ $50,000   ☐ $100,000
                ☐ $_____

Pastor Lang, as the Lord enables, I'll send monthly support of:

☐ $25.00   ☐ $50.00   ☐ $100.00 ☐ $500.00
            ☐ $_____

Pastor Lang, I know you and your family live by faith and mission support. I'll send mission support for you or Craig, or for the names of the other staff at the ranch.

Mission support for:

Name_____
$_____

Share alike with the present staff $_____

☐ Send names of staff in need of support.

We are a 501 (C) 3 organization and will send you a letter of thanks along with a receipt so you can use it for a tax deduction.

Please make all checks payable to:

Apache Creek Deaf and Youth Ranch

Pastor Lang leveling the land for a cabin.

Pastor Lang and church boys pouring cement floor for a cabin.

Pastor and Janice Lang.

Pastor Craig and Debbie Lang along with their three children: Rebekah, James and Bethany. Pastor Craig is the camp Director and Co Pastor of the church.